T0292915

The Strategic Planning and Deployment Excellence System (SPADES)

The Strategic Planning and Deployment Excellence System (SPADES)

Ensuring Complete Success from Strategic Plan Development to Deployment

Jack B. ReVelle, Ph.D.,
Susan L. Stuffle, PE, MBB
Harry K. Jackson, Jr., MBB

Routledge
Taylor & Francis Group
A PRODUCTIVITY PRESS BOOK

First edition published in 2020
by Routledge/Productivity Press
52 Vanderbilt Avenue, 11th Floor New York, NY 10017

2 Park Square, Milton Park, Abingdon, Oxon OX14 4RN, UK

© 2020 by Jack B. ReVelle, Susan L. Stuffle, and Harry K. Jackson

Routledge/Productivity Press is an imprint of Taylor & Francis Group, an Informa business

No claim to original U.S. Government works

Printed on acid-free paper

International Standard Book Number-13: 978-0-367-33301-0 (Hardback)
International Standard Book Number-13: 978-0-429-31988-4 (eBook)

Visit the Taylor & Francis Web site at
www.taylorandfrancis.com

The authors dedicate this book to our respective families for their enduring support and patience, not only during the writing process, but for everything that has brought us to this point in life to make the creation of this book possible.

We also dedicate this book to all of you who read it, and value quality as a way of the future. Thank you.

Contents

Acknowledgments xi
About the Authors xiii

Chapter 1   SPADES: What Is It and Why Use It? 1
               Implementing SPADES 3
               Honolulu Surfers: Implementation of SPADES 5

Chapter 2   SPADES Roles and Responsibilities 7
               Critical Functions of an Enterprise 7
               Roles and Responsibilities for Implementation of
                   SPADES 10
               Honolulu Surfers: SPADES Roles and Responsibilities 12

Chapter 3   Preparing for Strategic Planning 15
               Current State Assessment 16
               Customers and Their Needs and Wants 19
               Future State Estimate 20
               Honolulu Surfers: Preparation for Strategic Planning 22

Chapter 4   The Strategy Planning Retreat 25
               SWOT Analysis 27
               Organizational Needs Matrix 27
               Force Field Analysis 28
               Strategic Plan 30
               Honolulu Surfers: Strategy Planning 32

Chapter 5   The SPADES X-Matrix 37
               X-Matrix Legend 37
               X-Matrix Template 39
               Honolulu Surfers: X-Matrix Construction 40
               Deployment 44

Chapter 6   Developing the Strategy – SPADES Steps 1–3 45
               SPADES Step 1: Establish Organization Vision 46

SPADES Step 2: Develop Long-Term Goals............................48
SPADES Step 3: Develop Annual Objectives 50
Honolulu Surfers: Implementing SPADES
    Steps 1–3 52

Chapter 7   Deploying and Implementing the Strategy –
SPADES Steps 4–5..57
SPADES Step 4: Deploy/Roll Down to Departments
    to Develop Plans 58
SPADES Step 5: Implementation 61
Honolulu Surfers: Implementing SPADES
    Steps 4–5 66

Chapter 8   Progress and Annual Reviews – SPADES
Steps 6–7 71
SPADES Step 6: Progress Review (Monthly and
    Quarterly) 72
SPADES Step 7: Annual Review 75
Honolulu Surfers: Implementing SPADES
    Steps 6–7 78

Chapter 9   Reviewing and Refining the Strategy 85
Review of Prior Year (or Other Determined Period)
    Accomplishments 86
Roles and Responsibilities for the Review
    Meeting 88
Refine the Strategy..91
Honolulu Surfers: Reviewing and Refining
    Strategy..92

Chapter 10 Organizational Challenges and Cures 97
1. Strategy 98
2. Leadership 100
3. Personnel 106
4. Data 110
SPADES Self-Analysis Checklist..113

Chapter 11 Epilogue 119

Appendix A

SPADES Summary 123
Step 1: Establish Organizational Vision 123
Step 2: Develop Long-Term Goals 124
Step 3: Develop Short-Term and Immediate
      Objectives 125
Step 4: Deploy/Roll Down to Departments to
      Develop Plans.. 126
Step 5: Implementation.. 127
Step 6: Progress Review 128
Step 7: Annual Review 129

Appendix B

Potential Tools to Use with SPADES.................................. 131
  1. Affinity Diagram 131
  2. Arrow Diagram 133
  3. Catchball Model 134
  4. Cause and Effect Analysis 135
  5. Current State Analysis 136
  6. Force Field Analysis.. 137
  7. Future State Estimate 138
  8. Interrelationship Digraph 139
  9. Kano Model... 141
10. Organizational Chart.. 142
11. Organizational Needs Matrix 143
12. Pareto Chart.. 144
13. Performance Dashboard.. 144
14. PERT Chart... 146
15. Process Decision Program Chart 147
16. Project Selection Matrix.. 148
17. Risk Management Matrix... 150
18. Run Chart.. 151
19. Senior Management Review Checklist......................... 152
20. Strategy Deployment Tools... 153
21. SWOT Analysis 155
22. X-Matrix Tool 156

Index 157

Acknowledgments

As with writing any book there are several people who deserve special recognition. First, thank you to our families. Their support and encouragement made this book possible. Thank you to R. Sean Baron who helped us understand the structure and relationships necessary to bring the Honolulu Surfers to life. The publishing and editing team at Taylor & Francis, especially Michael Sinocchi and Katherine Kadian: we appreciate their support and forbearance, without which this book would not have been possible.

About the Authors

Jack B. ReVelle, Ph.D.
A Consulting Statistician
Cactus_Statman@yahoo.com
www.ReVelleSolutions.com

Dr. Jack B. ReVelle provides his advice and assistance as a consulting statistician to manufacturing and service companies throughout the U.S., Great Britain, Australia, and China. Better understanding and continuous improvement of his clients' processes and systems are accomplished through the application of a broad range of Lean Six Sigma-related tools, techniques, and methods. Dr. ReVelle also provides his technical assistance as both a quality and an industrial engineering expert to attorneys in litigation.

His credentials include over 40 clients, over 80 webcasts, and over 30 books, handbooks, videos, and software packages including *Safety Training Methods* (2nd edition), the *Mechanical Engineers Handbook* (3rd edition), the *Manufacturing Handbook of Best Practices: An Innovation, Productivity, and Quality Focus, The QFD Handbook, Quality Essentials: A Reference Guide From A to Z,* and, most recently, the *Home Builder's Guide to Continuous Improvement: Schedule, Quality, Customer Satisfaction, Cost, and Safety.*

Dr. ReVelle has been a judge for the RIT – *USA Today* Quality Cup and a member of the Board of Directors for the Arizona Governor's Awards for Quality. Sponsored by the American Society for Quality (ASQ) between 2010 and 2018, Dr. ReVelle developed and presented over 80 webcasts on Lean Six Sigma, Total Quality Management and Continuous Improvement tools and methods. He is a former member (twice) of the Board of Examiners for the Malcolm Baldrige National Quality Award, a judge for Arizona Governor's Awards for Quality, and a member of the Awards Council for the California Governor's Award for Quality.

Dr. ReVelle received his B.S. in Chemical Engineering from Purdue University, and both his M.S. and Ph.D. in Industrial Engineering and Management from Oklahoma State University (OSU). Prior to earning his Ph.D., he served 12 years in the U.S. Air Force. During that time, he was promoted to the rank of major and was awarded the Bronze Star Medal while stationed in the Republic of Vietnam as well as the Joint Service Commendation Medal for his work in quality assurance and nuclear safety with the Pentagon-based Defense Atomic Support Agency (DASA).

In 2006 Dr. ReVelle was inducted into the Purdue University ROTC Hall of Fame and awarded the Oklahoma State University College of Engineering, Architecture and Technology (CEAT) Lohmann Medal. He is a three-time Fellow having been elected by: the Institute of Industrial and Systems Engineers (IISE), the American Society for Quality (ASQ), and the Institute for the Advancement of Engineering (IAE). He is listed in *Who's Who in Science and Engineering, Who's Who in America, Who's Who in the World*, and as an Outstanding Educator in *The International Who's Who in Quality.*

Dr. ReVelle was awarded the Dorian Shainin Medal by the ASQ in 2012 and the Simon Collier Quality Award by the ASQ-Los Angeles Section 700 in 2015. In 2016, Dr. ReVelle was inducted into the Oklahoma State University CEAT Hall of Fame and the OSU Cowboy Academy of Industrial Engineering and Management. He authored the lead article for the 50th anniversary issue (November 2017) of ASQ's *Quality Progress* journal. Most recently, Dr. ReVelle was honored by the ASQ Orange Empire Section 0701 as its first ever "Quality Guru" in December 2017.

All told, Dr. ReVelle has had multiple careers. Starting as a chemical engineer in 1957, he has been a U.S. Air Force explosive ordnance disposal (EOD) officer, an aerospace statistician, a university professor, a university administrator, a safety consultant, a consulting statistician, an author, and an editor. He has been a local, regional, and national officer in the American Society of Safety Engineers (ASSE), the Institute of Industrial and Systems Engineers (IISE), the American Production and Inventory Control Society (APICS), and the American Society for Quality (ASQ).

Susan L. Stuffle, P.E.
United States Marine Corps Engineer/Analyst
Certified Lean Six Sigma Master Black Belt
susanstuffle@gmail.com

Susan Stuffle is a career Navy and Marine Corps civilian with over 27 years of experience in process improvement. Ms. Stuffle joined the USMC Lean Six Sigma/Continuous Process Improvement (LSS/CPI) core team at Headquarters, Marine Corps, in September 2006, where she served as a Lean Six Sigma Black Belt in the National Capital Region. She transitioned to the West team in July 2008, was certified as a Lean Six Sigma Master Black Belt in 2013 and supported Marine Corps LSS/CPI activities in the West region until 2015. In 2015 she became one of two Senior Master Black Belts leading the Lean Six Sigma program at Marine Corps Installations Command, and in 2018 she will hold the same role with Marine Corps Logistics Command. During the five years prior to her LSS/CPI engagement, she led the Business Engineering Team at Naval Facilities Engineering Command Southwest, based out of San Diego, CA. This team supported Headquarters Marine Corps, via the "Marine Corps Business Enterprise" in the areas of best practice analysis, process analysis and assessment, performance measures development, strategic planning, and other business engineering requirements.

Ms. Stuffle is a U.S. Marine Corps certified Master Black Belt, Villanova University Master Black Belt, and American Society for Quality (ASQ) certified Black Belt. She has taught thousands of students, supported hundreds of process improvement projects, mentored practitioners, and co-authored many of the Marine Corps' Lean Six Sigma strategic guidance documents and templates, including training curriculum. She has also earned the Theory of Constraints (TOC) Jonah certification through the AGI Goldratt Institute.

Ms. Stuffle is a cum laude graduate, receiving a Bachelor of Science degree in Industrial Engineering from the University of Arizona in 1990 and a Master of Business Administration degree from the University of Texas at Dallas in 2007. She has worked for General Dynamics, Convair Division, and Hughes Aircraft, Missile Systems Group, in the areas of quality assurance and environmental engineering. Her civilian Navy career has included Public Works Management support in the areas of service contract technical development, regional acquisition strategies, technical training, strategic sourcing support, and policy development; Environmental Engineering support in the areas of remedial project management and environmental compliance; and Business Engineering support in the areas of performance management, analysis, and strategic planning.

Ms. Stuffle has completed coursework in Environmental Compliance with the University of California, San Diego. She is a certified Professional Engineer with the state of California, has been a member of the Society of American Military Engineers (SAME), is currently a member of the American Society for Quality, and a Senior member of the Institute of Industrial and Systems Engineers (IISE). In addition to performance and achievement awards, Ms. Stuffle has received a Navy Meritorious

Commendation Medal and was selected as Naval Facilities Engineering Command, Southwest Division, Business/Support Line Employee of the Year in 2005. She was awarded USMC LSS/CPI Project of the Year by the Commandant of the Marine Corps in 2010. Perhaps most importantly, Ms. Stuffle is the dedicated wife of CAPT Doug Stuffle (USN), and mother of two wonderful sons, LTJG Nathan Stuffle (USN) and 2nd Lt Caleb Stuffle (USAF).

Harry K. Jackson, Jr.
HarryKJackson@gmail.com
www.harrykjackson.com

Mr. Jackson is an internationally recognized author, lecturer, and consultant in the development of Quality & Reliability Programs in government and industry. He has over 30 years of experience in manufacturing, engineering, quality management, and Naval Engineering. During his career he has served in many different leadership positions: physicist, engineer, program analyst, director of testing, department manager, and executive vice president. This experience covers a wide range of government and commercial organizations. He is also a retired Naval Commander with extensive experience in management of Naval engineering activities and projects.

Mr. Jackson has trained, facilitated, and provided consulting services in the application of Lean Six Sigma, Quality, Reliability and Management tools and principles. He has designed, developed, and instructed numerous seminars on Quality and Management techniques for San Diego State University, University of California, as well as government, business, and industrial organizations with focus on both industrial production and service requirements.

He developed and led the implementation of Lean Six Sigma programs for several government and civilian organizations: United States Marine Corps; American Ordnance LLC; Armaments Research, Development and Engineering Center (TARDEC-ARDEC); ARMY PEO Ammunition; and many Army Suppliers. He supported McDonnell Douglas's implementation of Quality Improvement and Lean programs to reduce the cost of the C17 aircraft production – which resulted in the implementation of structured quality and reliability programs that significantly reduced production costs and helped position them to win the Malcolm Baldrige National Quality Award.

Mr. Jackson developed the Enterprise Excellence concept providing a holistic methodology for leading organizations to achieve the competitive advantage through establishing a culture of Continuous Process Improvement. These efforts have realized savings for the U.S. Army and its suppliers in excess of $40 billion, and the first Lean Six Sigma self-sustaining organization (Armaments Research, Development, and Engineering Center) which was the first DoD recipient of the Malcolm Baldrige National Quality Award.

Mr. Jackson has been a speaker and lecturer at the First Congress of Central American Industrial Engineering Students, Institute of Industrial and Systems Engineers, American Society for Quality, and many others. He developed and presented a Quality Engineering curriculum for the General Staff of the Egyptian Air Force. He used Quality Function Deployment and Hoshin Kanri to assist the reorganization of the Egyptian Air Force Maintenance system. Mr. Jackson has innovated and led the application of Design for Lean Six Sigma tools for designing and developing the Marine Corps Recruiting Command Organization Resource Analysis Process, the U.S. Marine Corps Radar Regionalization System, and the Army's new Squad Automatic Weapon.

Mr. Jackson holds a Bachelor of Science Degree in Physics. He is also a graduate of the Six Sigma Academy. His publications currently include: *Enterprise Excellence; Fulfilling Customer Needs; Achieving the Competitive Edge: From Concept to Customer*; and *The Leader.* These books have received broad acceptance as demonstrated by reviews and translations into Spanish, Portuguese, and Chinese.

1

SPADES: What Is It and Why Use It?

The distinguished economist Joseph Schumpeter once wrote, it is difficult to stay competitive in an economy where new customer requirements and new technologies constantly undermine the value of investments in old technologies and business processes. This is more evident today than ever before. In the past couple of decades there have been changes in technology and the way business is conducted that a few short years ago would have only existed in the world of science fiction and fantasy. These developments have changed the way business is conducted and the way manufacturing is performed. These developments, in some instances, have proven technical limitations not to be limitations at all. The current rapidly changing business and technology environment has altered, and continues to markedly alter, the face of local, national and international business, industry, and government. Continued long-term success in this environment requires flexible and agile strategic planning. Furthermore, these plans require regular periodic monitoring, evaluating, and adjusting consistent with changes in the technological and business environment as well as customer requirements.

In the past, the normal way to ensure competitiveness has been to hire capable people and fire them if they fail to meet the financial objectives of the enterprise. Recognizing the need to meet the challenges of customer satisfaction in an environment of accelerated changing technology and customer requirements, the Japanese developed "Hoshin Kanri" as an operating system. Hoshin Kanri integrates all aspects of the enterprise: sales, marketing, engineering, manufacturing, supply chain management, and customer service. Hoshin Kanri turns "management by objectives" to "management by means," thereby forcing a systems approach to leading and managing the enterprise. Of course, it is relatively easy to agree on goals such as better products, higher revenues and lower costs; it is much more difficult to agree on the "means" to accomplish those goals. With means, tradeoffs are required among business functions, suppliers, and even customers. This operating system provides Japanese business and industry with the flexibility and agility in strategic planning to meet the challenges of accelerated changes in technology and customer requirements.

The Strategic Planning and Development Excellence System (SPADES) provides a path to long-term success in this environment of rapidly changing technology and business systems. SPADES is the integration of the best of Hoshin Kanri, Quality Function Deployment (QFD), and other proven management and leadership tools and techniques. It innovates the application of these tools and techniques and creates the methodology of SPADES. The result is a methodology that guides the development and deployment of a long-term plan for achieving sustained success. These concepts within SPADES ensure the strategic planning process traces from the foundation of organizational principles to the enterprise vision and to the organization's long-term goals. This methodology leads to the establishment of short-term goals and objectives, then to short-term tactics, improvement objectives, and activities. Ultimately this methodology leads to the establishment of responsible actionees, resource requirements, anticipated deployment costs, and a prioritized deployment plan of action and milestones.

The Scientific Method is the foundation upon which the tools and techniques of SPADES are applied. The Scientific Method begins with an observation of a phenomenon which leads to development of a hypothesis to explain the phenomenon. The hypothesis is then tested and, based on the analysis of the results, the hypothesis is accepted or adjusted as necessary. The testing may then be repeated to verify conclusions. The Deming-Shewhart Cycle of plan–do–check–act (PDCA) is the application of the Scientific Method for control and continual improvement of processes and products. SPADES is the integrated evolution of the PDCA Cycle and QFD to answer the challenges of how to stay competitive, year after year, in a dynamic environment of rapidly changing customer requirements and technology.

Unexpected consequences can derail the strategic plan as easily as any short-term plan.

The law of unintended consequences has been recognized as a part of economics, politics, and sociology for centuries. It is the result of not carefully evaluating a course of action and exploring all potential consequences. Robert Merton, an American sociologist, in his 1936 article

"The Unintended Consequences of Purposive Social Action," identified five sources of unanticipated consequences for human activity:

1. *Lack of Knowledge.* Insufficient data prevents accurate identification of consequences. Proper planning requires fact-based decisions which is only possible if all critical factors are explored, data are collected, and confidence levels are understood for the data.
2. *Error.* Accurate and statistically valid data analysis is critical for developing correct information for decisions about consequences. If it is not it will lead decision makers to erroneous decisions about consequences.
3. *Imperious Immediacy of Interest.* The desire for the intended consequences is so great decision makers purposefully ignore any unintended effects.
4. *Basic Values.* The planned action is a direct result of the fundamental values of the decision makers and so the possibility of any unintended consequences is ignored.
5. *Self-Defeating Predictions.* The knowledge of the prediction of the intended consequences and of the action inspires individuals to change behavior and thereby changes the resulting consequences.

IMPLEMENTING SPADES

SPADES Provides a Sound Methodology for Developing a Strategic Plan and Avoiding Complications from Unintended Consequences

The successful plan will be accomplished by carefully managing consensus decision making during all phases of the process. This ensures the key staff and support personnel have a stake in the process and the plan. They then become the cadre of supporters for deploying the plan. The planning process begins with identification of personnel for developing the plan, support personnel, and resources for supporting the development. It is critical that they understand the SPADES methodology. The next step is for the team to establish a clear understanding of the vision, mission, and core values of the organization. This will be followed by a plan to ensure the vision, mission, and core values are deployed throughout the organization and that missions/charters for organizational elements are collaborative and supportive.

Data Collection is Critical for Preparing to Develop a Successful Strategic Plan

As the vision, mission, and core values are identified the planning team develops the requisite data requirements for developing the enterprise specific Strategic Plan. This will include data requirements for a Strengths–Weakness–Opportunities–Threats Analysis (SWOT) as well as critical enterprise performance metrics, and other identified critical planning data. Once the data requirements are established a data collection plan is established and implemented to collect the data for establishing the strategic plan. Throughout this data collection process, it is critical that performance metrics are collaborative and supportive of the values, vision, mission, goals, and objectives.

Deploying the Strategic Plan is a Process

The SPADES planning team ensures metrics are collaborative and supportive for the deployment and that the measuring methodology is appropriate and valid. The strategic plan establishes roles and responsibilities for deployment and for monitoring, measuring, evaluating, and reporting progress. The plan needs to include a Communications Plan for reporting progress and celebrating success. Depending on the specifics of the plan, regular periodic progress reviews need to be performed and reported monthly. Some of the elements of the plan may only need to be evaluated quarterly, however, the strategic plan is critical for long-term success and therefore needs to be a major part of managing the enterprise.

Reviewing the Strategic Plan Deployment ensures success.

What gets measured gets done and what gets reported gets done quicker. Successful deployment of the strategic plan requires regular, periodic measurement and evaluation of deployment progress. Based on the regular periodic reviews the plan can be adjusted so as to keep it appropriate for the business climate and technological changes. The results of the evaluations need to be communicated in accordance with the Communications Plan of the Strategic Plan.

HONOLULU SURFERS: IMPLEMENTATION OF SPADES

Throughout this book, the Honolulu Surfers baseball organization scenario will be used to demonstrate the implementation of SPADES. The organization consists of the imaginary Honolulu Surfers Major League Baseball (MLB) team which is supported by farm teams. Each team has an owner whose primary goals include earning a profit, winning games, and making the fans happy and enthusiastic about each of the teams. The leadership of each team, as illustrated in Figure 1.1, is focused on supporting the goals of the owner of their team. In order to achieve success for the entire Honolulu Surfer organization it is critical that each team's goals and objectives align, and all members of each organization performs collaboratively in support of the entire organization.

In future chapters, look for the Honolulu Surfer icon, for practical examples of steps and tools as we progress through the SPADES model.

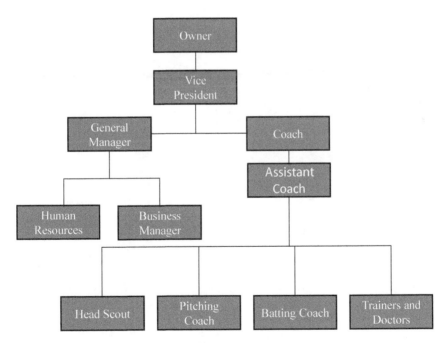

FIGURE 1.1
MLB Staff and Farm Team Organization.

2

SPADES Roles and Responsibilities

There are numerous definitions for "enterprise" ranging from "a unit of economic organization or activity, especially a business organization" to "a systematic purposeful activity." Whichever definition you accept, every enterprise, no matter how large or small, whether business, industry, academic, healthcare, or government, starts with a vision. This vision is normally supported by a mission statement and set of goals. So as to achieve the vision and the supporting goals eight critical functions are employed.

CRITICAL FUNCTIONS OF AN ENTERPRISE

Strategic Planning

In Chapter 1 the need for strategic planning and deployment was established to ensure an organization's long-term survival and ability to thrive. Successfully achieving the vision and mission requires an organization's leadership team to develop and deploy their enterprise values, vision, mission, goals, and objectives in the Enterprise Strategic Plan. This plan documents the direction for the organization. It provides the foundation for the structure of the enterprise as well as the roles and responsibilities of each function and the workforce within each work center.

Market Research, Customer Research, and Communications

This function develops the data that identifies the customers and their expectations and requirements, and measures customer satisfaction. This information provides the basis for establishing which technology to pursue, as well as what products and services to offer. It is also used to develop customer and marketplace communication strategies.

Research and Technology Development

Research and Technology Development identifies and develops technologies to improve the efficiency and effectiveness of both the operations and administration. It also develops technologies to assist the Product, Service, and Process Design function.

Product, Service, and Process Design

This function includes identifying and defining differentiating characteristics for the products and services, and then designing the products and services to meet customer requirements and expectations. This function also includes the implementation of the processes to produce the products and services. These operations are supported by the processes of Market Research, Customer Research and Communication, as well as Research and Technology Development.

Product and Process Commercialization

This function includes selection of materials, design of production processes, make–buy decisions, and variability reduction activities. It also includes all of the supplier selection and Supplier Quality activities.

Product and Service Production

This function includes all operations necessary to produce the products and services after initial development. This function requires close coordination with Research and Technology Development; Product, Service, and Process Design; Product and Process Commercialization; as well as Product and Service Support. Research and Technology Development facilitates the development of effective and efficient production processes. Product, Service, and Process Design ensures the necessary operational processes are implemented to support the production of the products and services. Product and Process Commercialization ensures purchased materials, parts, and supplies meet cost, schedule, and quality requirements. Product and Service Support collects, analyzes, and reports service information and customer feedback to improve production operations.

Product and Service Support

After the product or service is delivered to a customer, there are continued opportunities to serve the customer. The nature of these support activities will depend on the "mission" of the enterprise. These may include repair, maintenance, order tracking, exchanges, and other service functions critical to customer satisfaction. These activities also provide an opportunity to collect further information about customer wants and desires. This function has direct, post-production connection with the customers and suppliers. Thus, the data collection and analysis of Product and Service Support needs to coordinate with the other seven critical functions.

Measurement, Analysis, and Knowledge Management

This function provides the policies, guidelines, and requirements for selecting, collecting, and integrating data and information. It establishes the key enterprise performance metrics, and provides for regular periodic performance reviews. Data collection (measurement) and analysis develops information about various aspects of the enterprise. The application of information yields knowledge. The application of knowledge creates wisdom. The effectiveness of the previous seven functions depends, therefore, on the accuracy, quality, reliability, and availability of data and information.

These eight functions are critical for the long-term survival and thriving of the enterprise. How these eight functions are organized and relate to each other will depend on the size of the organization and its mission. The organization will include several levels of operations and administration. This structure will align as the Executive Staff which includes the President/Owner/CEO of the enterprise and his/her direct reports, e.g., assistants, division heads, department heads, and subsidiary presidents. Each of these executives will have direct reports, e.g., section heads, branch heads. Next there will be positions that will be analogous to Supervisor, or Lead. And reporting to these supervisors will be operators, technicians, or other process operators. Given the potential complexity of the structure of the organization it is important to establish the roles and responsibilities for the full implementation of SPADES.

In order to achieve the vision, mission, and goals of the enterprise a series of metrics needs to be established, measured, collected, evaluated, and reported at all levels. These metrics need to be collaborative and supportive so the activities throughout the organization can be aligned to evaluate progress and ensure achievement of the goals. At the operational level performance metrics evaluate the efficiency of the processes. These also include metrics of performance quality and timeliness. At the midlevel, i.e., departments, branches, and divisions, the metrics need to measure the effectiveness of their operations and rolled up to the executive level. At the executive level the metrics are measures of the enterprise performance in achieving the vision, mission, and goals. It is critical that every individual in the organization understands the vision, mission, and goals of the enterprise. It is also imperative that they understand how their responsibilities are collaborative and supportive to the long-term success of the enterprise.

ROLES AND RESPONSIBILITIES FOR IMPLEMENTATION OF SPADES

SPADES provides a clear path to long-term success. The roles and responsibilities for implementation of SPADES are structured to ensure success.

Chief Executive

The implementation of SPADES begins with the decision by the Chief Executive, i.e., President, Owner, or CEO, to fully adopt SPADES. This requires a commitment to follow through with the process and prioritize Strategic Planning. The Chief Executive is the face of the organization's mission, vision, and strategy. Whether or not he or she is involved in the day-to-day engagement of the strategy, the organization needs to clearly see the Chief Executive as the leader of the strategy. This person participates in annual planning meetings, and opens up key meetings with the Executive Staff and even with the extended field staff, on occasion. The Chief Executive appoints a Facilitator for SPADES. At the conclusion of each year, the Chief Executive is prominently engaged in annual reporting meetings, as well as summaries of results, feedback to the organization, and celebrations of successes.

Executive Staff

Subordinate executives in the organization are the conduit from the Chief Executive to the rest of the organization and back. They engage their direct reports in strategy planning, ensure that the Chief Executive is aware of current and planned activities associated with the strategy, make critical directional decisions for their areas of responsibility. Each member of the Executive Staff will be responsible to conduct planning meetings for their organizations. They are responsible for ensuring that the members of their organizations understand the Strategic Plan and develop the necessary processes, metrics, measurements, analysis, and reporting for accomplishing the SPADES Plan. It is recommended that the executive staff member introduce the meeting and then use a SPADES Facilitator to facilitate the meeting. This will ensure the staff members understand the importance of the Strategic Plan. The Executive Staff member can fully participate in the meeting and the organization members, in participating, instead of being led by "the boss," will develop a shared ownership in their part of supporting the Strategic Plan. At the conclusion of each year (either fiscal or annual), the Executive Staff is prominently engaged in annual reporting meetings, as well as summaries of results, feedback to the organization, and celebrations of successes.

Managers and Operational Leaders

With respect to strategy planning and engagement, managers and operational leaders hold roles similar to that of Executive Staff, but cascaded through to the next level(s) of the organization.

Operational Leaders

In addition to above, operational leaders must ensure that workers are engaged in, and accomplishing, what has been laid out in the organization's strategy. These leaders are the direct link between field activities and management. They are much like chameleons, in that they can align themselves to represent the perspective of workers when communicating to management, and can represent management when communicating with workers. The operational leaders must thoroughly understand the organization's mission, vision, and strategy, and support that strategy, in order for the organization to succeed.

SPADES Facilitator

The role of the SPADES Facilitator is to fully understand the strategy planning process, as well as the Chief Executive's vision for the enterprise. The SPADES Facilitator ensures that the supporting research and data collection for the planning meetings is accomplished. The Facilitator conducts the planning meetings and facilitates the planning. This allows the Chief Executive to participate in the planning meetings rather than driving the meeting, which facilitates the participation of the Executive Staff members. This critical tactic ensures ownership by the members in the plan results. They will not only be responsible for deploying the Strategic Plan within their areas of responsibility, but will, by virtue of their ownership in the plan, be the principle salespersons for the plan.

Depending on the size and complexity of the organization, the Strategic Plan is thereby cascaded down in a waterfall fashion. Each organization will develop its appropriate actions and metrics to support the deployment of the plan. Once the plan is fully implemented, regularly scheduled reviews will be conducted to evaluate progress and develop recovery plans, as necessary. These will then be rolled up in reverse to the planning waterfall.

HONOLULU SURFERS: SPADES ROLES AND RESPONSIBILITIES

Returning to the organizational chart introduced in Chapter 1, we can now link each position displayed in the chart to the roles and responsibilities described in this chapter (see Figure 2.1).

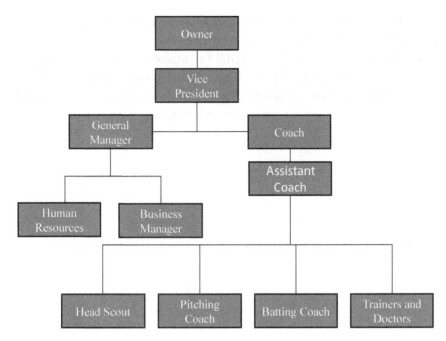

FIGURE 2.1
MLB Staff and Farm Team Organization.

- *Chief Executive.* The Owner of the Honolulu Surfer's organization serves as the Chief Executive. He made the decision to engage in strategic planning and specifically to adopt the SPADES approach to strategy planning and development, and, of course, implementation. In the following chapters his commitment and follow-through will be displayed as the Honolulu Surfers' scenario unfolds. The Owner is clearly the leader of the strategy.
- *Executive Staff.* The Vice President, General Manager, Coach, and Assistant Coach serve as the Honolulu Surfers' Executive Staff. They participate in the organization's annual offsite to initiate planning and engage their direct reports in strategy planning and deployment. At the conclusion of each year, the Executive Staff is prominently engaged in annual reporting meetings, as well as summaries of results, feedback to the organization, and celebrations of successes.
- *Managers and Operational Leaders.* The managers and coaching staff of the Honolulu Surfers and its farm teams serve as the next level of engagement for SPADES. They are the link directly to players, field staff, and office staff. Their commitment and engagement are the

direct link to actions by staff that will lead the organization toward achievement of the Chief Executive's vision.

- *SPADES Facilitator.* The SPADES Facilitators are not on the organizational chart, but will be discussed throughout the scenario, highlighting the value of third-party facilitation support when engaged in planning, working sessions, and reporting.

3

Preparing for Strategic Planning

What are the key components of any strategic plan? They are usually the Vision, Mission, and Core Values of the organization which are supported by the outputs of the organization. These key components should ensure that they take into account the current state of the organization and business environment, the customer's needs and wants, the business environment scan, and an estimate of the future state. This is shown in Figure 3.1.

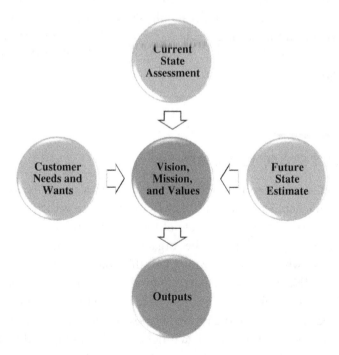

FIGURE 3.1
Strategic Plan Components.

Note: Many government entities prefer to use the term "end user" or "beneficiary" in place of "customer."

Strategic Planning requires the leadership of the organization to develop a vision of itself at some future time. Strategic planning is a long-range big picture perspective of the organization that is designed to provide guidance and direction to the organization. For each organization "long range" is defined by its vision and the realities of its operating environment, e.g., changing technologies, budgeting cycles, competition, and customer demographics. For most organizations long range is usually five years, since it is far enough out that fact-based estimates can be made for the future, but close enough to the current state to make modifications as necessary to ensure flexibility and agility to meet changes in its technical and operational environment. The strategic plan is really a model that simulates the path to achieve the stated vision and shows how the organization will exist and function in this future environment based on a number of rational assumptions. In addition, this model shows, at a high level, the resources required so as to function successfully in the future. The model should also identify who the major *customers* will be and what their needs and wants will be in this future state.

Preparation for the strategic planning session involves the following three steps.

CURRENT STATE ASSESSMENT

Agreement on the starting point, in order to build a future, is essential in preparing for a strategic planning session. The first step is therefore to thoroughly understand the current state of the organization, i.e., the organizational profile. Leadership of the organization must make an honest assessment of where the organization is at this point in time in relationship to its vision. This includes an analysis of products, workforce, suppliers, and more. This is a vital first step since it is necessary to understand the current strategic position and the organization's position in the marketplace. Frequently, complete and accurate data is not available to support this analysis. If this is the situation, educated guesses (supported by experience) may be used with an explanation of how it was developed, including an estimate of the confidence in its accuracy. This analysis is the baseline that all who are attending the strategic planning session agree to in advance. Valuable time at a strategic planning session should not be spent debating the current state of the organization. This needs to be done in advance and agreed to by all attending. The leader of the strategic planning session needs to develop a draft of the current state and circulate it to obtain feedback and then use the feedback to develop a consensus. This may require a few pre-meetings, but you can be certain it will be a worthwhile investment.

The Malcolm Baldrige National Quality Award (MBNQA), the gold standard for quality and performance assessment of organizations, recommends including the following organizational characteristics for developing an organizational profile. These characteristics are broken into the following categories:

1. *Organizational Environment.* This category addresses the facts, meaning what is being created by the organization, what are the guiding documents, how many people are on-hand, what is the financial situation, and what regulations are involved. In order to better understand and document these facts, MBNQA offers the following questions as a guide:

   a   Product Offerings

   What are your main product offerings?

   What is the relative importance of each to your success?

   What mechanisms do you use to deliver your products?

   b   Mission, Vision, and Values

   What is your stated mission, vision, and values?

   What are your organization's core competencies, and what is their relationship to your mission?

   c   Workforce Profile

   What is your workforce profile?

   What recent changes have you experienced in workforce composition or in your needs with regard to your workforce?

   What are your workforce or employee groups and segments, the educational requirements for different employee groups and segments, and the key drivers that engage them in achieving your mission and vision?

   What are your organized bargaining units (union representation)?

   What are your organization's special health and safety requirements?

     d Assets

         What are your major facilities, technologies, and equipment?

     e Regulatory Requirements

         What is the regulatory environment under which you operate? What are the key applicable occupational health and safety regulations; accreditation, certification, or registration requirements; industry standards; and environmental, financial, and product regulations?

2. *Organizational Relationships.* This category addresses people and interactions in support of the facts just described by documenting how the organization is set up, who receives value and outputs of the organization, and who provides inputs to the organization. Again, MBNQA offers the following questions as a guide:

     a Organizational Structure

         What are your organizational leadership structure and governance system?

         What are the reporting relationships among your governance board, senior leaders, and parent organization, as appropriate?

     b Customers and Stakeholders

         What are your key market segments, customer groups, and stakeholder groups, as appropriate?

         What are their key requirements and expectations for your products, customer support services, and operations?

         What are the differences in these requirements and expectations among market segments, customer groups, and stakeholder groups?

     c Suppliers and Partners

         What are your key types of suppliers, partners, and collaborators?

         What role do they play in your work systems, especially in producing and delivering your key products and customer support services; and in enhancing your competitiveness?

         What are your key mechanisms for two-way communication with suppliers, partners, and collaborators?

         What role, if any, do these organizations play in contributing and implementing innovations in your organization?

         What are your key supply-chain requirements?

All data accumulated for the strategic planning session needs to be documented as being fact-based or opinion-based. Opinion-based data may simply be a best guess by a senior executive and may be as true as some of the fact-based data. Participants must be informed of each data source. This information is critical to understanding the accuracy of the data and its reliability. In addition to knowing the source, data must be screened as to its relevance to future planning. The relevance of the data should be ranked as high, medium, or low and indicated as such on each document to be used. Understanding the source and reliability of data will enable the analysis to turn the data into usable information that can be applied to develop "wisdom" about the Strategic Plan development and deployment.

CUSTOMERS AND THEIR NEEDS AND WANTS

One of the most important pieces of data for the strategic planning session is a clear understanding of the organization's customer base. The customer base needs and wants must be fully understood. This understanding can be accomplished by surveys, customer contacts, field reports, sales people's knowledge, etc.

The Kano Model, as described in Figure 3.2, is a tool used to graph customer needs and wants, increasing understanding from the limited descriptions provided by customers, to a more in-depth assessment based on three levels as documented by the model. The first and most basic level is known as the "Expected" level, and is the minimum description of customer needs, usually addressing reliability and durability needs. The second level is the "Wants" and addresses issues of performance of the product or service provided. This is an area where the organization can begin to differentiate itself from the competition. The third level is the "Exciting" level, where an organization builds in features or functions not expected by a customer, delivering superior performance when compared to the competition. While a baseline Kano model is useful, it is important to understand that, over time, Exciting migrates to Wants and then finally to Expected. Kano Models must be updated on a regular basis due to the changes in customer needs and wants, and also the competitive environment. The classification system of the Kano Model can be used when preparing for the strategic planning session, as a way to compare and contrast the organization's performance compared to its competitors in each category.

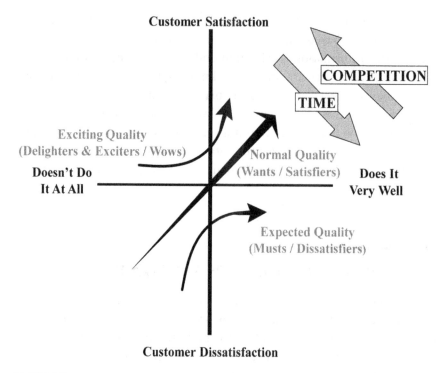

FIGURE 3.2
Kano Model of Customer Needs.

Customer satisfaction is the result of delivering a product or service that meets customer requirements, needs, and expectations. It is determined by how well the performance delivered matches the customer's expectation. Only when this is done well will the organization build a loyal customer base upon which to grow. It is imperative to develop a continuous measuring and monitoring process at various customer "touch points" so as to provide valuable input for an organization to constantly understand their customer's satisfaction with products and services.

FUTURE STATE ESTIMATE

Once the current state is accurately described and the data to support that description has been gathered and analyzed it is now appropriate to make an estimate of what the future state of the organization could look like. This can be drafted by the senior staff prior to the strategic planning session. The important aspects of the future state include:

- What are the underlying factors driving the organization into the future?
- What are current factors that work for the organization today that might change? How much and in what direction (positive and negative)?
- What are the consequences of underestimating future trends?
- What technological changes could have the most impact and what will it cost to meet those challenges?
- Who will be our major competitors in the future and what are their strengths and weaknesses?
- Who will be our customers and what will they demand?
- What workforce competencies will be required and what is the gap between current workforce competencies and future needs?
- How will these trends be monitored, and what will be the reaction to any changes?

This is just a sampling of the questions that could be asked to define the future state the organization will be operating in while trying to achieve its strategic plan. For some organizations it might be a short time horizon (less than three years), for others it may be longer (five years or greater). Whatever the time horizon, it is imperative to have a monitoring system in place that is tracking and reporting how these important aspects of the future state are unfolding so adjustments can be made if the direction changes or the pace accelerates or decelerates. The organization must be quick to see the forces of changes and react accordingly.

Strategic planning should be used to provide future direction. Strategic planning is for mature, stable organizations and not for an organization in crisis which usually requires immediate action and very short-term planning. The strategic planning process should force the leadership of the organization to think strategically, and not operationally, about the future. Operational thinking is more inward and not future oriented.

HONOLULU SURFERS: PREPARATION FOR STRATEGIC PLANNING

1. *Current State Assessment.* The Honolulu Surfers' management has developed a simplified Current State Analysis, Figure 3.3, in preparation for strategic planning.

2. *Customers and Their Needs and Wants.* Honolulu Surfers identified customer needs and wants by conducting a Kano Analysis. This revealed that the customer fan base is satisfied with an average winning season and would be excited by division and league championships. The top delighter, of course, would be to win the World Series. Owner and Advertiser Kano Analyses are in agreement with the fans, but for differing reasons. Fans are seeking excitement, while Owners and Advertisers seek revenue and longevity.

3. *Future State Estimate.* The Honolulu Surfers' management has also drafted a simplified Future State Estimate, Figure 3.4, in preparation for strategic planning.

   Having completed the basic preparation work for SPADES, the Honolulu Surfers organization is now ready to conduct their strategic planning offsite. Stay tuned, this will be discussed in the next chapter.

HONOLULU SURFER ORGANIZATION SIMPLIFIED CURRENT STATE ANALYSIS	
ORGANIZATIONAL ENVIRONMENT	
(1) Product Offerings	
What are your main product offerings?	Entertainment, Advertising Revenue, Merchandise
What is the relative importance of each to your success?	50%, 25%, 25%
What mechanisms do you use to deliver your products?	Live, Television, Streamed Video, On-line, Brick-and-Mortar Stores, Supplier to External Stores
(2) Mission, Vision, and Values	
What are your stated mission, vision, and values?	Mission: Honolulu Surfers, Winning games and riding the wave into the hearts of our loyal fans.
	Vision: We will surf the pipeline all the way to the World Series.
	Values: Fans first. Hang loose. Strong and steady.
What are your organization's core competencies, and what is their relationship to your mission?	Strong defense (pitching and fielding). Steady offense (batting and running).
(3) Workforce Profile	
What is your workforce profile?	See Figures in Chapter 1.
What recent changes have you experienced in workforce composition or in your needs with regard to your workforce?	New farm team and pitching staffs.
What are your workforce or employee groups and segments, the educational requirements for different employee groups and segments, and the key drivers that engage them in achieving your mission and vision?	See Figures in Chapter 1.
(4) Assets	
What are your major facilities, technologies, and equipment?	Surfer Stadium, Television and Cable agreements, Fan stores, and contracts with External Stores
(5) Regulatory Requirements	
What is the regulatory environment under which you operate?	MLB regulatory requirements, Salary caps, OSHA
ORGANIZATIONAL RELATIONSHIPS	
(1) Organizational Structure	
What are your organizational leadership structure and governance system?	See Figures and discussion in Chapter 1.
What are the reporting relationships among your governance board, senior leaders, and parent organization, as appropriate?	See Figures and discussion in Chapter 1.
(2) Customers and Stakeholders	
What are your key market segments, customer groups, and stakeholder groups, as appropriate?	Fans, Owners, and Advertisers
What are their key requirements and expectations for your products, customer support services, and operations?	Win games, win hearts, and grow fan base in order to grow revenue.
What are the differences in these requirements and expectations among market segments, customer groups, and stakeholder groups?	All involve increasing fan base in order to increase attendance, viewership, and merchandise sales.
(3) Suppliers and Partners	
What are your key types of suppliers, partners, and collaborators?	Honolulu Surfers organization, Farm Team organizations, MLB, broadcasters, advertisers, fans.
What are your key mechanisms for two-way communication with suppliers, partners, and collaborators?	Contracts and agreements.

FIGURE 3.3

Honolulu Surfers' Current State Analysis.

HONOLULU SURFER ORGANIZATION SIMPLIFIED FUTURE STATE ESTIMATE	
What are the underlying factors driving the organization into the future?	Fan base growth, resulting in revenue growth.
What are current factors that work for the organization today that might change? How much and in what direction (positive and negative)?	Farm teams and pitching staffs have adequate results, but we are looking into making changes to improve standings.
What are the consequences of underestimating future trends?	May miss opportunities to acquire new talent: players and staff.
What technological changes could have the most impact and what will it cost to meet those challenges?	Transmission and relaying of games and highlights will change with technology. Important, but secondary is sales technology for fan gear.
Who will be major competitors in the future and what are their strengths and weaknesses?	Current champions will continue to be major competitors, but aging players and salary caps are weaknesses for them, while strengths for Surfers (with younger players, smaller salaries).
Who will be customers and what will they demand?	Customers demand increasing trend in winning; access to transmission of games and highlights; variety and quality of fan gear.
What workforce competencies will be required and what is the gap between current workforce competencies and the future need?	Build stronger coaching staff; seek steady source and better processes than other teams for identification of new talent.
How will these trends be monitored, and will be the reaction to any changes?	Measurement of spring training and actual results.

FIGURE 3.4
Honolulu Surfers' Future State Estimate.

4

The Strategy Planning Retreat

This chapter does not discuss good general meeting planning techniques such as adequate, comfortable space, visual aids, use of technology, timely invitations, available transportation, and planning for some relaxing evening activities. These normal meeting planning techniques are assumed to be in place within the organization and will, without doubt, be executed flawlessly for the strategic planning retreat.

The purpose of conducting a strategic planning session is to engage the organization's leadership. It is critical that the senior leadership and the Board of Directors plan the future of the organization. Leaders must feel ownership and become committed, accountable, and responsible for the future strategic direction. Seneca, the Roman Philosopher, stated "If you know not what Harbor you seek, any wind is the right wind." If we do not have a strategic plan as established by leadership, the organization will drift along, following any course, possibly leading to irrelevance or failure.

Note: Rather than "marketplace," government entities may be seeking to understand the future "mission" or "campaign."

To develop a solid platform for leadership engagement in a strategic planning retreat the first step is to get the senior leaders on the same page. This can be accomplished by having a briefing book or materials prepared and delivered to them about a week before the scheduled retreat. The briefing book should contain the material that was discussed in the previous chapter, organized in a manner that takes the reader from the current state of the organization, to the assumptions for the near and long term, and then to a clearly stated conclusion about the future *marketplace* in which the organization will be competing, based on the preparatory analysis.

In addition to the briefing book some organizations hold background sessions for the first two to three hours at the start of the strategic session. One way to do this is to staff the meetings with the "knowledge experts" who accumulated the data, while dividing the executives into teams that rotate every 30 minutes to a new group. The senior executives can question these knowledge experts on notes they may have made in their briefing books. The smaller rotating groups allow time for more questions and a deeper understanding of the issues to be discussed during the strategic planning retreat. The knowledge experts present facts and do not set future policy. These knowledge experts are usually on call during the strategic planning retreat if some data interpretation is required or more data needs to be developed. The background sessions can be modified and used as the strategic plan is deployed through the organization, so the next level of leadership can see the data that supports the new strategic plan.

In addition to background sessions, some organizations have a keynote speaker, who is widely viewed as an industry expert, to discuss the current marketplace and what is seen developing or unfolding for the foreseeable future. Industry experts bring an air of authority to the discussions, especially if they are held in high regard by the senior leaders attending the retreat. *Recording the keynote speaker address is a good idea in order to use the recording as part of the deployment process for the next level of leadership and beyond, expanding overall knowledge of the industry.*

Another possible presentation before the retreat begins is to focus on the customer experience. This can be done by presenting quality data on how products or services are performing for the customer. Discuss recent customer surveys and what these surveys show as the organization's strong and weak points. In addition, it is a good idea to illustrate major competitors' strong and weak points in contrast to the organization's in order to determine where the organization is ahead and behind the competition. Some organizations may have a major customer attend who presents how they view the organization's products and services. However it is done, a clear and honest picture of how customers view the organization needs to be established.

SWOT ANALYSIS

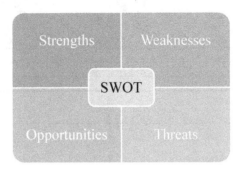

To start the retreat off it is important to present a summary of the strengths, weaknesses, opportunities, and threats, the organization is facing as it moves into the future. This is the time to gather input from everyone attending the retreat, summarizing results in a visual format for participants. This can be accomplished by dividing the group into teams, with each one taking one of the four categories to discuss and embellish. Then the individual groups report to remaining groups, allowing those in the other groups to provide their input.

ORGANIZATIONAL NEEDS MATRIX

Once background work is complete, it will be time to begin developing the strategic plan. The participants need to answer the following question: Based on what we have heard today, what are the most pressing organizational needs at this time? In addition to articulating and documenting the most pressing needs, a matrix (see Figure 4.1) should be developed to show how those pressing organizational needs are impacting the following:

- People – the organization's employees
- Processes – the primary processes of the organization
- Performance – improving efficiency and effectiveness of the organization

NEEDS	PEOPLE	PROCESSES	PERFORMANCE	CULTURE	MORALE	CUSTOMERS	OTHER	NOTES
Need 1	H	H	M	L	M	H		
Need 2	M	H	M	L	H	H		
Need 3	L	L	L	L	H	H		

FIGURE 4.1
Organizational Needs Matrix.

- Culture – creating a cohesive and aligned organization
- Morale – improving attitudes and satisfaction of employees, i.e., esprit de corps
- Customers – improving satisfaction of customers
- Other categories relevant to the organization.

The matrix needs to have a rating scale (such as high, medium, or low) so the impact of each need can be assessed. Comments to support each rating need to be captured. This matrix should be reviewed later in the retreat to ensure that the new strategic plan addresses and minimizes the greatest impacts on the organization.

FORCE FIELD ANALYSIS

Once the most pressing organizational needs are developed and agreed to, the next step is to document the forces of change and their velocity that will impact the organization in the future. The data presented in the earlier briefings will be the basis to develop this content. The forces of change can be arranged in a "Force Field Analysis" diagram that will show those forces that will positively and negatively impact the organization and their velocity of change as shown in Figure 4.2.

The left side of Figure 4.2 is where the positive forces of change are listed. Positive forces of change are ones the organization can use to drive

HOW?	WHY?	POSITIVE		NEGATIVE	WHY?	HOW?
			F O R C E S O F C H A N G E			
		STRENGTH (L, M, H)		STRENGTH (L, M, H)		

FIGURE 4.2
Force Field Analysis.

or facilitate the strategic direction. Negative forces of change are listed on the right side of the matrix and are ones that will restrain or inhibit the organization from reaching its future desired strategic direction. Each force of change listed should be evaluated as to its strength and a scale such as high, medium, or low (H, M, or L) should be developed for the participants to use in order to gain consensus. The high positive strength forces of change can be utilized to drive the organization forward and should be capitalized upon wherever possible in the organization. The high negative strength forces of change may require investment of organizational resources to overcome or minimize their impact on the strategic plan. The medium forces of negative change may only need to be monitored to ensure they do not become stronger. The impact of medium positive and negative forces of change upon the organization will vary from organization to organization and industry to industry. The monitoring process will also vary. The low positive forces of change are enablers to the strategic plan and should be incorporated into the organization deployment wherever possible. The low negative forces of change are usually easy to overcome and just represent a minor obstacle to the organization's progress.

Depending on what processes are chosen to communicate the data to the attendees, the most pressing organizational needs should be developed, and document the forces and velocity of change that will impact the organization in the future; anywhere from a half to a full day may have been consumed at this point. The next step is to begin to develop the strategic plan, building on the information that has been discussed and documented thus far.

STRATEGIC PLAN

The goals of an excellent strategic plan are:

- To focus the organization on the future and show the road map to that future state. A clear focused future vision guides the actions of all members of the organization.
- To help align the organization to the current and future enterprise goals and targets. This is the catalyst for the development of lower-level aligned action plans to achieve the goals. This process gets the whole organization pulling in the same direction at the same time. This will also help to align employee's daily work with what is important to the organization. Another goal of alignment is to inspire the workforce to purposefully participate and help move the organization forward.
- To help the organization as a whole understand its strengths and weaknesses. The strategic plan should show how the strengths will be maximized and how the weaknesses will be minimized.
- To show stakeholders the stewardship of resources that have been entrusted to the leaders of the organization. A clear, well focused strategic plan will make the stakeholders feel more comfortable in the leadership and the direction of the organization.

The key components of any strategic plan should include a clearly articulated vision of what tangible results the organization needs to achieve to remain a viable competitor in their defined marketplace and the timeline for those achievements. Once the results are defined, the next step is to understand the gaps between the current reality and future vision. The sizes of the gaps need to be understood and a consensus developed so that the appropriate resources can be made available to close the gaps. In other words, is there organizational commitment to closing these gaps directing the organization to where it should be in the future?

As the strategic issues are developed and vetted before the attendees, they need to be tested to make sure they are really strategic. Some simple questions to confirm strategic issues include:

- Is the issue of major importance to the future of the organization?
- Is the issue strategic or operational in nature?
- Does the issue build on the current strengths of the organization? If so, how?
- Is the issue forward looking and focused on the organization's defined area of business? If so, how? If not, why?
- Will it expand the business? If so, how?
- Is it credible or pie in the sky? Why?
- Will this issue improve internal and external customer relations? How?
- Will this issue energize the organization? How?

With every strategic issue that is developed, goals for the short term (1–3 years) and the long term (3–5 years) need to be developed. When developing these goals, the strategic retreat attendees must balance the sometimes-conflicting demands of the need for both short- and long-term results, and the wants and needs of varied constituencies served (stake-holders, customers, and employees). These short- and long-term goals, once developed, will be the input to the SPADES Matrix, discussed in the next chapter.

The strategic planning retreat should end with an action note that gets the momentum going with the senior leadership. Too often, par-ticipants leave the retreat with lots of good ideas that need to be final-ized over the next couple of months and then a lull sets in that sometimes is hard to overcome. It takes time to develop the official documents from the retreat but there are usually a number of issues that can be acted upon quickly. How to energize the leadership team to start moving forward? The answer is to leave the retreat with action items to start implementing. The retreat and future supporting meetings should always produce a plan of action and milestones (POA&M) with assigned responsibilities. To develop some of the initial short-term action items, ask the follow questions:

> Based on the knowledge gained during this strategic planning retreat, what does the organization need:
>
> 1. "To Start" doing to be positioned strategically for the future? Why?
> 2. "To Stop" doing to be positioned strategically for the future? Why?
> 3. "To Continue" doing to be positioned strategically for the future? Why?

Usually there will be a few items in each category that can be acted upon quickly. The retreat attendees should be divided up into teams to address each of the items. The teams will then meet during the following week to develop a near-term action plan for the items that can be implemented within a month. One month later the teams should meet to discuss and document actions and results. By setting a monthly meeting cadence in a short time, many small but important items that will facilitate the way to the future can be implemented. This keeps the momentum going while the meetings transition to strategy deployment and progress reviews.

HONOLULU SURFERS: STRATEGY PLANNING

In order to develop a sound, long-term strategy for the organization, the Senior Stakeholders (Owner(s), Vice Presidents, Managers, and Coaches) in the Honolulu Surfers organization agreed to participate in a Strategy Planning Offsite, separating themselves from the daily tasks of the organization and focusing on long-term planning. In preparing for the Strategy Planning Offsite, the Honolulu Surfers management staff assembled briefing books for all attendees, containing the Current State Assessment, Customer Needs and Wants, and Future State Estimate (as described in the previous chapter). Electronic versions of the documents were forwarded by the Owner to all attendees ahead of the Offsite, with instructions to review the materials and bring their questions to the Offsite.

In a surprise move, the Owner decided to hold the Offsite at his home, instantly setting the tone of the working session to a warm and open environment. The living room was set up with comfortable chairs and couches, light refreshments to the side, easels and chart paper placed in four corners of the seating area, with a wide bay window overlooking the Pacific Ocean.

The Owner brought in facilitators to help the discussions run smoothly and stay on task. As attendees arrived, the first few minutes were filled with greetings and casual conversations. Once the group was seated, the Owner opened the working session with a sincere explanation of the importance of long-term planning. The Honolulu Surfers had been somewhat successful in the past, but it was time to strive for more. It was time to stretch what had been considered boundaries and plan the true future of the organization. Expectations were high, and everyone agreed it was time for the Honolulu Surfers to reach a new level.

The facilitators stepped up to initiate the planned agenda.

1. *Introductions.* Although most everyone knew each other, there were a couple of new faces in the group, and the facilitators provided a brief background in order to begin developing a relationship with the group and establish a level of credibility and trust.
2. *Briefing Books.* Hard copies of the materials that had been sent as read-ahead were passed out, along with note paper and pens. A brief period of time was designated for questions and comments. All discussion items brought up by the attendees were listed by the facilitators on chart paper, visible to all. Anything that was not resolved during discussion was noted for further action.
3. *SWOT Analysis.* In order to plan for the future, the group needed to have a collective understanding of the current Strengths, Weaknesses, Opportunities, and Threats (see Figure 4.3). Placing these words at the top of clean pieces of chart paper, the group politely called out their thoughts regarding the Honolulu Surfer organization. Additional ideas were documented, the group prioritized the lists and noted the most important entries by placing an asterisk (*) beside each.
4. *Customer Surveys.* The facilitators handed out customer surveys further expanding the information provided by the Kano Analysis.

FIGURE 4.3
Honolulu Surfers' SWOT Analysis.

After providing a quick summary of the results, the attendees were allowed a few minutes to read for themselves.

5. *Needs Matrix*. With the background work complete, the facilitators asked the question: "Based on what we have heard today, what are the most pressing organizational needs at this time?" The group turned their attention to a hand-drawn table placed on the back wall of the room. The resulting Needs Matrix (Figure 4.4) was developed.

IMPACT: High, Medium, Low

NEEDS	PEOPLE	PROCESSES	PERFORMANCE	CULTURE	MORALE	CUSTOMERS	NOTES
1. Higher Division and Championship goals	High	Medium	High	Medium	High	High	
2. Retain players	High	Medium	High	High	High	Medium	
3. Strengthen pitching	Medium	High	High	Low	Medium	Medium	
4. Grow media component	Low	High	Medium	Medium	Low	High	
5. Improve minor league and farm team connection	Medium	High	High	Medium	Medium	Medium	

FIGURE 4.4
Honolulu Surfers' Organizational Needs Matrix.

6. *Force Field Analysis.* Based on the top five identified needs, the group then documented forces for and against addressing the needs (Figure 4.5).

7. *Develop the Strategy.* With all of the groundwork complete, adequate break times, plenty of refreshments, it was then time to get to the main event: Developing the Honolulu Surfer's Strategy. This is also the beginning of the official SPADES 7-Step Process, addressed in Chapters 6 through 9. We will save the Honolulu Surfers' next steps for the scenario details in those chapters. Keep on reading!

HOW?	WHY?	POSITIVE		NEGATIVE	WHY?	HOW?
Keep winning.	Retain players; increase profits; increase pay.	Current Winning Trend (H)	A D D R E S S	Higher salaries elsewhere (H)	Other teams have more $.	More established.
					Key position.	Better offers.
Media and internet opportunities.	Technology gains; younger viewers.	Lots of media opportunities (H)		Competition for pitchers (M)		
			F I V E	Changing technologies for media (M)	Changeover costs.	Select one and then change to another.
Keep current and increase loyal staff.	We are a family.	Dedicated and Loyal Coaches and Staff (H)	N E E D S	Dispersed minor and farm teams (M)	Communication and processes need maturing.	More experienced teams may take advantage.
		STRENGTH (L, M, H)		STRENGTH (L, M, H)		

FIGURE 4.5
Honolulu Surfers' Force Field Analysis.

5

The SPADES X-Matrix

Even a great strategic plan with brilliant long-term goals will collapse when it isn't fully deployed throughout an organization. Deployment of the plan is absolutely necessary so everyone in the organization, and even many stakeholders external to the organization, completely understand their respective responsibilities as they relate to the organization's mission, vision, and value statements which support the long-term goals. Everyone must know what to do, how to do it, when to do it, and why to do it.

Thus, SPADES, the Strategy Planning and Deployment Excellence System, was conceptualized and placed into practice. The SPADES X-Matrix discussed in this chapter is an integral part of creating a great strategic plan.

When a special team has been charged by executive management with the design and construction of a strategic plan, of necessity the team should be multi-level and multi-functional. The team should be conversant with the organization's mission, vision, values, and long-term goals as it begins its work. As part of a team's responsibilities, an X-Matrix should be created.

X-MATRIX LEGEND

Let's begin our examination and understanding of SPADES and the SPADES X-Matrix with a legend that facilitates comprehension of the X-Matrix construction process. There are six categories, five correlation matrices, and four correlation symbols. An example is provided for each category, correlation matrix, and correlation symbol.

Categories

[A]: *Long-Term Goals/Strategies.* These are intended to assist an organization in reaching the goals stated in the organization's vision. Example: A major league professional baseball team wants to win the World Series.

[B]: *Short-Term Goals.* These are the intermediate steps that will lead the organization to achieve its Long-Term Goals. Example: The team wants to win its league championship within three years.

[C]: *Short-Term Tactics/Improvement Objectives/Actions.* These are the steps the organization intends to take so as to achieve the Short-Term Goals. Example: Purchase or trade for five new players before the next season begins.

[D]: *Improvement Items.* Now we're getting into the nitty-gritty specifics of the steps the organization intends to take to achieve its Short-Term Goals. Example: Obtain the following players: one starting pitcher who has won at least ten games each season for the last five seasons; one relief pitcher who saved at least ten games last season; two outfielders who have at least 0.280 batting averages for the last five seasons; and one first baseman who has at least a 0.290 batting average and is great at defense (won at least two Golden Gloves within the past five seasons).

[E]: *Actionees/Accountable Persons.* These are the individuals who are responsible and accountable for on-time achievement of the Short-Term Tactics and/or Improvement Items, e.g., Team Owner, Team General Manager, Team Manager, Team Captain, Pitching Coach, Batting Coach, and Starting Catcher.

[F]: *Expenses per Action.* These are the financial resources necessary to accomplish each of the Short-Term Tactics, e.g., required travel costs and value of personnel time.

Correlation Matrices

It is important to understand the relationships between the entries in each category:

- To ensure everything is addressed, i.e., nothing is left out;
- To clearly understand where the more significant linkages occur.

The X-Matrix provides an easy to document and easy to understand assessment of these relationships via the Correlation Matrices:

[A × B]: Correlations between Long-Term Goals [A] and Short-Term Goals [B].

[B × C]: Correlations between Short-Term Goals [B] and Short-Term Tactics [C].

[C × D]: Correlations between Short-Term Tactics [C] and Improvement Items [D].

[C × E]: Correlations between Short-Term Tactics [C] and Actionees [E].

[C × F]: Correlations between Short-Term Tactics [C] and Financial Expenditures [F].

Correlation Symbols

The correlation symbols within each correlation matrix are used to annotate the strength of each category entry as it relates to the entries in the next category. The following symbols are used to indicate the strength of these relationships:

[>]: Indicates a strong correlation.
[=]: Indicates a moderate correlation.
[<]: Indicates a weak correlation.
[0]: Indicates no correlation.

X-MATRIX TEMPLATE

Figure 5.1 introduces the X-Matrix template.

The strategy planning sequence begins immediately below the boxed X in Section 1 which is where the Long-Term Goals [A] are placed. Remember, these goals are drawn directly from the organization's vision. Teams entrusted with using the SPADES X-Matrix are encouraged to limit the quantity of long-term goals to somewhere between three and five. Using more than five goals could lead to an overly complex X-Matrix that could easily result in discouraging the SPADES team members and/or making it difficult to explain to non-team members.

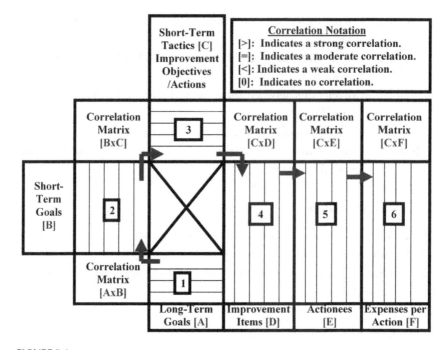

FIGURE 5.1
X-Matrix Template.

HONOLULU SURFERS: X-MATRIX CONSTRUCTION

The content in the examples below link to our scenario. Follow along, to see how the Honolulu Surfers strategic plan content fits into the X-Matrix.

The SPADES X-Matrix is a visual summary and analytical tool for all key components of the strategy. By documenting correlation between key elements of the strategic plan, it becomes easier to understand how actions, objectives, and goals move the organization toward achieving its vision. Also, missing correlations alert the strategic planning team to weaknesses in the plan.

It may require weeks or even months to create and fully document the strategy and deployment plan, as summarized by the SPADES X-Matrix. This is achieved by selecting and correlating prioritized goals, tactics, improvement items, actionees, and expenses.

As already noted in the discussion of the X-Matrix template, start the process by listing Long-Term Goals [A] in Section 1 located immediately below the X.

Next, determine the Short-Term Goals [B] necessary to achieve [A] and record them in Section 2, the block to the immediate left of the X. Done correctly, there will be strong, positive correlations [A × B] between the Long-Term Goals [A] and the Short-Term Goals [B], with some stronger or weaker than others.

Some Short-Term Goals can address more than one Long-Term Goal. The correlation matrix (see Figure 5.2) located in the bottom left corner of the X-Matrix portrays the [A × B] linkages. Remember, when Long-Term Goals exist without corresponding Short-Term Goals, nothing happens.

Tactics are objectives/actions to cause changes/improvements which are recorded in Section 3, the Short-Term Tactics block, located immediately above the X.

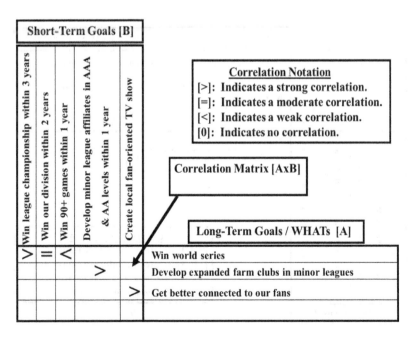

FIGURE 5.2
Honolulu Surfers' X-Matrix [A × B].

Correlations are tested again, but this time between the Short-Term Goals [B] and the Short-Term Tactics [C]. These are identified in the correlation matrix [B × C] located in the upper left corner of the X-Matrix (see Figure 5.3).

At this point the team records the process metrics [D] in Section 4, the Improvement Items block located to the immediate right of the X. The team then reviews the correlations; this time between the Short-Term Tactics [C] and the Improvement Items [D] located to the right of [C] and above [D] (see Figure 5.4).

In Section 5, located to the immediate right of the Improvements block [D], list the Actionees/Responsible Persons [E].

Next, the Improvement Items [C] are tied to the Actionees [E] in the Accountability correlation matrix [C × E] located above the Actionees [E] and to the immediate right of the Improvement Items [D] (see Figure 5.5).

The last major component is the Finances/Expenses per Action [F], located in Section 6 on the far-right side of the SPADES X-Matrix.

Finally, the Short-Term Tactics [C] are tied to the Finances/Expenses per Action [F] in the Finances correlation matrix [C × F] located in the top right corner of the X-Matrix (see Figure 5.6).

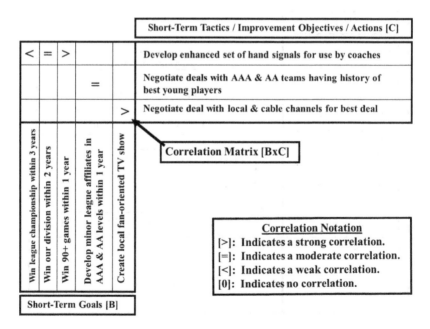

FIGURE 5.3
Honolulu Surfers' X-Matrix [B × C].

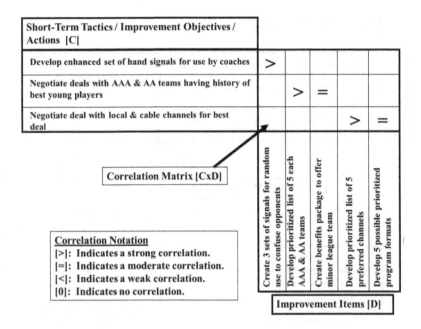

FIGURE 5.4
Honolulu Surfers' X-Matrix [C×D].

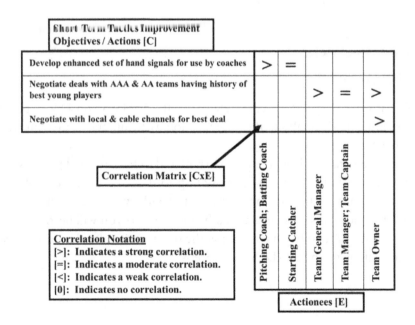

FIGURE 5.5
Honolulu Surfers' X-Matrix [C×E].

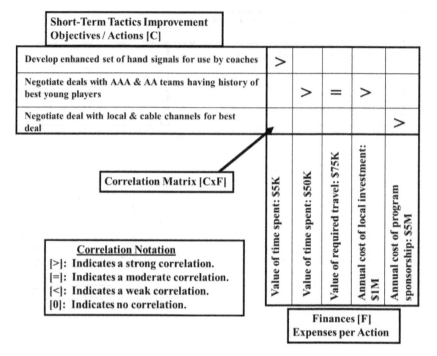

FIGURE 5.6
Honolulu Surfers' X-Matrix [C × F].

DEPLOYMENT

Now it's time to print the completed SPADES X-Matrix on 11 × 17 paper. Distribute it throughout the organization with all the leadership and associates.

It's important to keep the plan current and in full, internal public view. The plan is of little if any use if it's not up-to-date and easily accessible by those responsible for making it real. Just as with every other technique or tool, the more this process is used, the more expert you will become.

Now it's time to begin converting the organizational vision into a strategic plan using the SPADES Seven Steps.

6

Developing the Strategy – SPADES Steps 1–3

The SPADES approach to Strategic Planning consists of seven primary steps, with supporting key features. The seven steps have been designed to provide organization leaders and facilitators with a set of simple guidelines for development of a robust long-term strategy. Over the years, many tools have been established to assist with strategic planning; however, a step-by-step roadmap to strategic success has been missing. SPADES is the answer. The SPADES Seven Steps can be applied to any organization, in any industry:

> SPADES Step 1: Establish Organization Vision
> SPADES Step 2: Develop Long Term Goals
> SPADES Step 3: Develop Short Term and Immediate Objectives
> SPADES Step 4: Deploy/Roll Down to Departments to Develop Plans
> SPADES Step 5: Implementation
> SPADES Step 6: Progress Review
> SPADES Step 7: Annual Review

The seven steps fall into three groups that will be discussed in this and the next two chapters. The first group is SPADES Steps 1–3: Vision, Goals, and Objectives. This is the true planning portion of the SPADES approach. After building or revising or even confirming (depending on the maturity of the SPADES program and the number of SPADES cycles completed by the organization) a solid Vision statement supported by goals and objectives, the output of SPADES Steps 1–3 will serve as the foundation for the supporting activities during deployment and implementation of the strategy.

SPADES Step 1: Establish Organization Vision

SPADES Step 2: Develop Long Term Goals

SPADES Step 3: Develop Short Term and
　　　　　　　　Immediate Objectives

SPADES Step 4: Deploy/Roll Down to
　　　　　　　　Departments to Develop Plans

SPADES Step 5: Implementation

SPADES Step 6: Progress Review

SPADES Step 7: Annual Review

SPADES STEP 1: ESTABLISH ORGANIZATION VISION

During the Strategic Planning Session with leaders, as described in Chapter 4, the Vision for the organization is reviewed and revised, based on many factors, including current conditions, mission requirements, market trends, past performance, leadership priorities, and so on. All organizations have a Vision, whether or not it is referred to by that name. Leaders have future plans or destinations for the organization as a whole. Picture the organization as a naval vessel, or a cruise ship in the ocean. The ship's Captain has a destination identified for a future port. The Vision is the future port of the organization. Even if the ultimate desire is to retain the status quo, with the ocean current, there is still action required to remain in place. Most organizations, however, have plans to improve: increase market share, lead in technological advances, be the brand of choice for a chosen demographic, or win wars.

All Vision statements by definition are long-standing, enduring statements of where the organization would like to go. But, as time passes, it is necessary to review and validate or revise the organization's Vision. All strategic planning, and SPADES steps in our case, look to the Vision as the foundation for everything that follows.

Key Features of SPADES Step 1

Vision statements don't just materialize out of thin air. A good Vision statement is validated with data and rigor. There are some critical features to consider during SPADES Step 1.

1. *Data Input from Internal and External Performance.* In order to understand the market or environment and the organization's position, data must enter the picture. Facts and numbers establish the current state, and the desired state of the organization. Data that is appropriate for consideration most likely is already collected by someone within the organization and should now be made available and visible for all leaders in the context of planning for the organization's long-term future.

2. *Customer Focus.* All organizations exist to serve end users, or customers. The Vision must be intent on providing or obtaining the best possible item, service, footing, advantage, experience (you fill in the noun for your organization). If the Vision is inversely focused solely on the organization, then the purpose of this exercise has been completely missed. Success is more likely with a Henry Ford attitude of "The man who will use his skill and constructive imagination to see how *much* he can give for a dollar, instead of how *little* he can give for a dollar, is bound to succeed."

3. *Environment Factors* (e.g., Social, Regulatory, Economic, etc.). The current and future environment play into the long-term vision of the organization. What was a social norm ten years ago may currently not be acceptable. Regulations today may increase or decrease tomorrow. The target market may find that customers transition from small amounts of expendable budgets to large and then back to small, given the changing economic environment. Norms, expectations, and a little luck play into planning for environmental factors associated with a long-term vision.

4. *Draft of Vision Reviewed with Organization for Reality Check.* Depending on the organization, a leadership retreat or planning session may be at risk of "group think." This is particularly true if time is short, lunch is next on the agenda, or there is another reason to rush to consensus on the Vision statement. It is always a good idea to expand the audience to a variety of interests for a reality check. Send the Vision Statement out to all or a sample

of the organization for honest feedback. Make sure to manage expectations and hold to a reasonable deadline. With the intent of keeping the Vision Statement short and easy to remember, participants in the review need to understand that this is not a wordsmithing exercise. The purpose of the review is to ensure that the ship is heading toward the right continent, not to specify the precise harbor.

5. *Finalized Vision Communicated Clearly to Everyone at All Levels.* Once the Vision is reviewed and validated or revised during the Strategic Planning Session (Chapter 4), it is published, forwarded, distributed, and made visible to *everyone* in the organization. This cannot be over-done. The Vision can be posted in hallways, on website headers, inside elevators, on letterheads, t-shirts, coffee mugs, anywhere and everywhere. Leaders should ask employees at all levels if they know the Vision of the organization. In order for everyone to work together to achieve the Vision, they first need to know what it is! How many organizations hide their Vision statements behind the covers of strategic plans that are sitting safe and sound (and unread) in the mahogany bookcases of the front office leaders? Unfortunately, this may be the norm. So, *market* the Vision to internal employees. Make the Vision short and direct, catchy and easy to remember, if possible. Then, base *everything* on that Vision. Ask everyone how their work can contribute to that Vision. Move to the next SPADES step.

SPADES STEP 2: DEVELOP LONG-TERM GOALS

By looking at least three to five years ahead, the organization can develop long-term goals to help everyone move along the path toward the Vision discussed above. These goals should be challenging, should stretch people's comfort levels and help to ensure the organization doesn't become complacent in "the way we have always done things." By continuing to look ahead, striving to be the best, the organization can remain aware of competition and reduce the risk of being left behind. Think of a company such as International Business Machines (IBM): the master of the computer universe in the 1980s. What happened? Did they not see changing technology? Were they not aware of the Visions and plans of their competitors? Computers are a bigger part of our lives now than they were back then. Why am I not typing these words using an IBM laptop? IBM was surpassed by competition, limping along in the 1990s until the Personal Computer division, including the ThinkPad laptop, was finally sold to China's Lenovo in 2005. Could IBM have done something different? Were their long-term goals flawed?

The three- to five-year objectives are not just significant due to time to achieve them. They should involve several parts of the organization. A single employee cannot complete one of these objectives alone. The complexity of a correctly written three- to five-year objective includes contributions by many members of an organization. But don't worry; we will get to individual contributions as we progress through the SPADES steps.

Key Features of SPADES Step 2

1. *Focus on the "gap" between your present organizational capability and required performance to reach the Vision.* This gap can only be determined by measuring the current state of the organization, using quantifiable data. How is the organization currently performing? What is the market share or readiness level or scoring in critical areas? Set the top level and mid-level leaders free to research this information. Have an honest conversation without retribution, with the understanding that true analysis can result in better future dividends than inflated positives.

2. *Accurate data from past performances determines present capability* of the organization and means to be pursued over the next three to five years. Once the organization knows where it currently stands, with factual information to back up that knowledge, it sets the stake in the ground regarding where to grow, what to achieve, how to change over the next three to five years to get closer to the all-important Vision. Think big! Very big!!! Three to five years can represent over 10 percent of a person's working career. It's a sizeable chunk. People want to make a difference. Challenge them to do so. Then give them the time and resources to be successful. This is discussed further in a later SPADES step.

3. *Communicate the long-term goals clearly to everyone at all levels.* As with the Vision, it is difficult to expect progress without

communicating goals to anyone and everyone. While the Vision is short and sweet, possibly catchy, the long-term goals create a better understanding of direction for everyone in the organization. They provide a target for which to aim. These goals need to be visible to employees: reviewed at staff meetings, accessible on-line, an input to annual performance planning and appraisals. They may not be memorized by all (like the Vision should be), but their general intent should be known, discussed, and a driver of activity.

The long-term goals help members of the organization to understand the general direction that will be taken in the quest toward achieving the Vision. By establishing these long-term goals, individuals can begin to understand where and how they may be able to contribute to erasing these "gaps" between the current state and where the organization would like to go. This makes it easier for the organization to develop annual objectives – which is the natural next step in SPADES.

SPADES STEP 3: DEVELOP ANNUAL OBJECTIVES

Annual objectives are the short-term goals that provide the action for reaching the longer-term goals. There is nothing flashy or surprising about this organized breakdown of planning. SPADES uses a proven, logical, methodical approach to guiding the ship so as to eventually arrive at the destination as described by the Vision and long-term goals. Once you become familiar with the SPADES steps, you may ask yourself: "Why isn't everyone already doing this? It's so simple and *obvious*." Yes, it is. But, like many things in life, it is easy to get lost in the fog of day-to-day activities and forget about or feel uncomfortable with long-term planning. By understanding this simple approach, the fog rolls away, and the horizon can be clearly seen. SPADES serves as the recipe for success.

Now that the Vision and long-term plans have been developed, how about taking a look at the shorter-term plans to make those long-term plans happen? Annual objectives that feed into and help to achieve the long-term goals must be established. Think about what can honestly be accomplished in a year, and also reverse engineer the long-term goals by planning what must be accomplished each year in order to achieve those goals, and what resources are required for success.

Key Features of SPADES Step 3

1. *Annual objectives are completely integrated with long term goals and Vision. Every* annual objective should link to an existing long-term goal. Rogue objectives simply can't be as important as those that directly support longer-term goals. Therefore, diverting resources to anything that doesn't line up with longer-term goals may unintentionally hurt chances for, or reduce, progress toward reaching those goals.

2. *Small number of focus points, fewer more important efforts vs. more, more, more.* Along the same line of thinking as featured above, too many annual objectives can also produce a negative result. In *Good to Great*, Jim Collins calls "good" the enemy of "great." Too many good things can consume all resources, preventing the great things from occurring. Annual objectives are critical for success. They are the connective tissue between strategic plans and tactical plans. Maintain vigilance to develop no more than what is essential and no less than what is essential when it comes to annual objectives.

3. *Accurate data, minimally filtered, is the basis for selecting one-year objectives.* All strategic planning needs to be based on facts, backed by data. But, at this mid-level of planning, data need not be perfect – it just needs to be available. Let's not get stuck at this point in our strategic planning by analysis paralysis. SPADES activities need to be top priority and revisited at appropriate frequencies for plans to remain correct and relevant. Metrics must be identified for long-term monitoring, building a historical picture of where the organization has been and progress that has been made, with the ability to transition to expectations for the future. A rush to collect data during the period of strategic planning is not the way to go. First, how reliable can this data possibly be? Can it show trends or seasonality? Will people be tempted to "fudge" some of the data in order to provide it in time? Data collection should be a constant and foundational part of running any organization. However, a balance must be achieved to ensure that the value of the data meets or exceeds the effort to collect it. As with annual objectives, collecting data on a few critical (great) metrics may be much more valuable than on many less critical (good) metrics.

4. *"Reason for improvement" must be compelling.* A convincing case must be made to work on any selected objective rather than on

something else. In order to strengthen the criteria for selecting annual objectives, look at the other side of the coin: in addition to ensuring that annual objectives tie to longer-term objectives, make the argument for why other activities are less important. As a good member of a debate team, argue for both why the annual objective should be selected and also why other actions should not be pursued. Be thorough and fact-based.

High-level, big picture planning is the bedrock of a successful organization, with employees and structures that align to support the ultimate goals of the organization. SPADES Steps 1 to 3 consist of the foremost planning elements that must take place in order to create an environment for alignment. The Vision and supporting long-term and short-term (annual) objectives serve as the foundation on which deployment or dissemination throughout the organization and implementation can be built. More on that in the next chapter!

HONOLULU SURFERS: IMPLEMENTING SPADES STEPS 1–3

Recall from Chapter 4, the Senior Stakeholders (Owner, Vice President, Managers, and Coaches) in the Honolulu Surfers organization were participating in a Strategy Planning Offsite, at the team Owner's home. All preliminary work had been conducted, including review of Briefing Books that contained the Current State Assessment, Customer Needs and Wants, and Future State Estimate, as described in Chapter 3. With the help of facilitators, the attendees developed a SWOT analysis, followed by the development and analysis of five primary needs of the Honolulu Surfer organization:

1. Higher Division and Championship goals
2. Retain players

3. Strengthen pitching
4. Grow media component
5. Improve minor league and farm team connection.

With the groundwork for strategy planning complete, it was time to develop the strategy.

SPADES Step 1: Establish Organization Vision

The facilitators wrote the vision on a large piece of paper in front of the room:

WE WILL SURF THE PIPELINE ALL THE WAY TO THE WORLD SERIES!

After much discussion, everyone agreed with the intent of the Vision. The performance, environment, and customer discussions that took place earlier during the Strategy Planning Offsite confirmed the vision. However, the consensus was that the vision could be improved and possibly shortened, making it simpler to remember, and hopefully integrated into signs, letterheads, and greetings among employees. Building on the concepts of baseball, World Series, sun and sand, the revised Vision was formed:

WORLD CHAMPIONS IN PARADISE

Everyone was pleased with the result but agreed not to get too set on the new phrase until there was time to circulate the Vision out to the rest of the organization for feedback.

SPADES Step 2: Develop Long Term Goals

The final action taken during the Strategy Planning Offsite was to draft the long-term goals for the organization. The group took the organizational needs described above and distilled them into measurable long-term goals to be accomplished over the next three to five years:

1. Win the World Series
2. Develop expanded farm clubs in minor leagues
3. Get better connected to our fans.

The goals were certainly challenging, and a bit outside the comfort levels for the leaders of the Honolulu Surfers organization. But, at the same time, the energy and excitement levels were clearly increasing. The room was abuzz with side discussions, laughter, and even a cheer!

As the facilitated Strategy Planning Offsite was brought to a close, the group was asked to think about the following three questions overnight, and be prepared to act on them when returning to the office the next day:

Based on the knowledge gained during this strategic planning retreat, what does the organization need? The answer was:

1. "To Start" doing to be positioned strategically for the future? Why?
2. "To Stop" doing to be positioned strategically for the future? Why?
3. "To Continue" doing to be positioned strategically for the future? Why?

Back at the office on the following day, the revised Vision and Long-Term Goals were circulated to those who didn't attend the offsite, and also was sent to the Managers and Coaches of the farm team organizations, with a request for feedback by the end of the week. In an unexpected move, the Owner personally visited his Honolulu Surfers players and staff and traveled to the supporting team sites to share the Vision with everyone, ensuring that the minor and farm team players and staff understood the vital role they play in the overall success of the Honolulu Surfers organization.

Positive response was overwhelming. Once received, the official feedback was ready to be reviewed. The members of the Leadership Team who participated in the Strategy Planning Offsite had already scheduled a working meeting. During the meeting, the group reviewed feedback and discussed near-term action plans based on the answers to the "Start, Stop, and Continue" questions that had been assigned as homework following the offsite. This leadership team agreed to meet monthly to continue to build the strategic plan and monitor progress toward the Honolulu Surfers' long-term goals and vision.

The organization's feedback was overwhelming. Everyone seemed excited about the clear and positive direction set by leadership. Signs and posters were immediately ordered and hung in hallways and elevators.

Also, to help everyone keep in mind the long-term goals of the organization, the following messages were posted around the offices and on every working level web-page:

ALOHA! What did you do today to help us:
* ***Win The World Series***
* ***Develop expanded farm clubs in minor leagues***
* ***Get better connected to our fans***

The following month, the second official Strategy Planning monthly meeting was held. Progress from the first month was reported, and it was time to expand planning to include Short-Term Objectives. What needed to be done in the next year or so to significantly move the organization toward meeting the Long-Term Goals?

SPADES Step 3: Develop Annual Objectives (Short-Term Goals)

During the monthly meeting, facilitators reviewed the Vision and Long-Term Goals with the Honolulu Surfers leaders. Everyone was reminded that every annual objective needed to tie to a three to five-year goal. Also, metrics would need to be identified to ensure that progress toward the goals could be understood and the goals eventually met. After developing many options for consideration, the leadership team settled on the following short-term objectives:

1. Win league championship within three years
2. Win our division within two years
3. Win 90+ games within one year
4. Develop minor league affiliates in AAA and AA levels within one year
5. Create local fan-oriented TV show.

Everyone agreed that the objectives were aggressive, and while they wouldn't be accomplished in a single year, they would definitely be possible in the next three years in support of the longer-term goal period of three to five years.

With the Strategic Plan contents settled, it was time to disseminate and implement! Continue on to Chapter 7 to see what happens next.

7

Deploying and Implementing the Strategy – SPADES Steps 4–5

Deployment of the strategic plan is all about line of sight from the strategy to the operational plan to the day-to-day execution of the activities that make the operational plan a reality. Many types of radio transmissions depend, to varying degrees, on line of sight between the transmitter and receiver. Obstacles that commonly cause non-line of sight conditions include buildings, trees, hills, mountains, and, in some cases, high-voltage electric power lines. Some of these obstructions reflect certain radio frequencies, while some simply absorb or garble the signals; but, in either case, they limit the use of many types of radio transmissions.

The most common non-line of sight obstacles that exist in deployment of the strategic plan are:

- Poor communications of the strategic plan throughout the organization
- Lack of believability that it can be achieved
- Poor selling job by senior executives on the importance of the strategic plan
- People in the organization are unable to connect their position, roles, and responsibilities to the strategic plan
- The plan just arrived and no one was told what to do with it
- No formal process of deployment and review.

The second group of SPADES steps includes SPADES Steps 4 and 5: Deployment and Implementation of Strategy. Following planning, an organization must disseminate and overcome both individual and collective inertia with respect to actions that will accomplish the objectives discussed in the previous chapter.

SPADES Step 1: Establish Organization Vision

SPADES Step 2: Develop Long Term Goals

SPADES Step 3: Develop Short Term and
Immediate Objectives

SPADES Step 4: Deploy/Roll Down to
Departments to Develop Plans

SPADES Step 5: Implementation

SPADES Step 6: Progress Review

SPADES Step 7: Annual Review

SPADES STEP 4: DEPLOY/ROLL DOWN TO DEPARTMENTS TO DEVELOP PLANS

All levels of an organization must adopt the line-of-sight approach to strategic deployment. Long-term goals and short-term objectives lead everyone in an organization to establish a connection, and a responsibility for intentional and specified actions that lead to achieving objectives that have been developed by leadership. This will ensure all functions are collaborative and supportive in implementing the strategic plan.

Key Features of SPADES Step 4

Deployment of strategy and objectives is where concept meets concrete planning. This is the transition from strategic to tactical documentation of actions; from academic to actual. This is the missing element resulting in most unsuccessful Strategic Plans. The strategies are often good, perhaps excellent, but the failure is in translating broader strategies to local actions. *The key features of Step 4 may be the most valuable content within this book.* By paying close attention and following this guidance, an organization can significantly increase the probability of successful strategic planning.

1. *Clear, disciplined action plans with direction for improvement, what is to be measured and processes to be improved.* Every single department and every single employee within the organization must have an action plan containing Specific, Measurable, Achievable, Relevant, and Timebound (SMART) actions. Some actions may task a group of employees, where others may be linked to a single employee or position. But remember, a task or action is not enough: actions need to be measurable, linked to one or a few critical metrics, to include time periods and due dates.

2. *Continuous give and take ("catchball") between levels, around chosen targets and an organization's capabilities.* While managers at various levels of the organization may initially draft actions for their departments and/or employees, by using the catchball method, those actions can be refined and improved through a combined effort between managers and subject matter experts (SMEs, i.e., the employees). The catchball approach, as shown in Figure 7.1, engages management and employees. It allows managers to retain decision authority while increasing engagement and input from employees. This is a scalable approach and can be used across multiple as well as single levels of the organization. The catchball model, as simply pictured, begins with management planning, tossed to employees for input, back to management for agreement or adjustment, and then possibly another round of employee input, until a solid plan with SME consensus is settled.

3. *Emphasize the plans of departments/units versus just individuals.* The waterfall or cascading effect for strategic planning involves

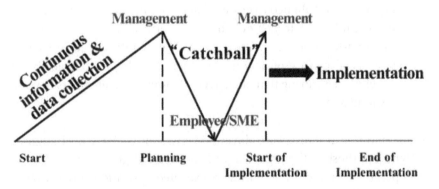

FIGURE 7.1
Catchball Model.

department-level objectives and actions, with a clear line of site for each and every employee, making his or her contribution relevant to the success of the entire organization. Be purposeful and vigilant with this element of Step 3. This is where many strategies miss a critical step, making it difficult and often impossible for employees to connect to the overarching strategy of the organization.

4. *Team coordinates plans across departments.* It is not enough for a department to look vertically at an organization's plans. In addition to understanding the higher-level objectives and linking to current level and lower-level actions, the head of the department must facilitate coordination horizontally across peer-level departments. Perhaps some work crosses department boundaries, or there is a dependency across departments. In order to fully understand and plan for success, communication and visibility across departments is a must.

5. *Responsibilities clearly designated.* As introduced above, actions must be SMART. A clearly written action is directly linked to one or more positions or individuals. Supporting responsibilities must be established and clearly understood by employees. This is where one-to-one communication between managers and employees, on a regular frequency, is imperative. Employees must understand their tasks, timelines, and associated metrics.

6. *The leadership team, with assistance from SPADES facilitators, also ensures the sum of plans are collaborative and supportive for achieving the vision.* All of this tactical work culminates in a consolidation effort, where the strategic planning team brings all of the pieces of the planning puzzle back together, drawing from all departments, to ensure sections and pieces are not missing. The resulting actions are organized and aligned to ensure that deployment planning can guide the organization to achieve the short-term objectives and thereby the long-term goals. By using the X-Matrix introduced in Chapter 5, a visual picture of actions and their correlation to objectives is developed, ensuring that objectives and important elements have not been missed.

A key question usually heard during deployment is "How do I align my activities to those of the organization?" Strategic alignment refers to how the operational and daily activities are executed in relationship to strategy and external environment. When alignment is attained the organization gains competitive advantage and increased performance.

Alignment of the strategic plan to the organizational operations involves the following which are facilitated by the use of the SPADES X-Matrix:

- Document the key drivers of the organization as to why the organization exists and is of value to its customers.
- Relate the key drivers to company mission and value through the SPADES X-Matrix.
- Identify executive level measures that are used or should be used to monitor and track the achievement of key drivers.
- Map operating unit goals and objectives to executive level measurements so that results roll up and show overall organizational progress.
- At the daily work management level, map personal achievements to operating unit goals.
- Identify any additional achievements to company goals beyond those of your operating unit and relate them to established measures.

To accelerate results, the senior leadership should spend less time defining the what and how of continuous improvement, and more time defining who and why. Engage people with an inspiring vision and connect their activities through aligned management systems. By pointing the organization toward a customer-centric future state and giving people the autonomy to change products, services, and processes to achieve their goals, the organization can exponentially increase its success.

SPADES STEP 5: IMPLEMENTATION

The strategic planning is finished. We are ready and aimed. Now it is time to fire. All of the work to this point is a *big waste of time*, if the plan is not implemented. And there is no proof of success without measurement. It is show time. With the vision known by all employees, weeks or months of planning and communicating complete, there is an atmosphere of excitement and determination as the entire organization readies for the start of a new period of implementation. This is a good time for the top leadership to bring all employees together, in a single room, or linked via video conferencing, to celebrate the beginning of the new strategic era. A sense of camaraderie in support of the success of the whole organization by the efforts of the many can be magnified with the right kick off. If resources allow, pass out personal items such as mugs or t-shirts, featuring the organization's vision statement.

Key Features of SPADES Step 5

It takes vigilant engagement and monitoring to ensure the organization performs as a collaborative and supportive team. The SMART actions and related objectives must be visible to employees, using a graphical representation of progress. Tables, pictures, and charts can be displayed in hallways, on websites, at regular status meetings. Daily tasks and fires must not divert attention away from the big picture of the organization's vision and objectives. It takes effort, but with strong leadership, a steady focus on strategy will prevail.

1. *Disciplined data collection and measurement system are implemented "in process," not after the fact.* With actions and metrics established, frequency of monitoring and assignment of monitoring duties known, the disciplined measurement begins. This is no time to become weak on accountability. The leadership team needs to ensure strict adherence to measuring, analyzing, reviewing, and reporting progress. Negative trends are dealt with in real time, with adjustments made before significant lapse in planned results can occur. Staff meetings at all levels of the organization include the standing agenda item of reviewing current measurements.

2. *Visible process (targets and means) allows for real time recognition and re-enforcement.* The Seven Quality Control (7-QC) Tools are excellent options for creating a visual measurement environment, e.g., Statistical Control Charts or Run Charts, updated at a regular frequency, can demonstrate progress and trends, or Pareto Charts with results by department may establish a healthy competitive vibe within the organization (see Figures 7.2 and 7.3). Achieving milestones on or ahead of schedule can be met with recognition and celebration. The energy and excitement level of the organization can grow in such a visible and positive environment.

3. *Standardized methods reduce some manager-to-manager variability in outcomes.* The strategic planning team or facilitators, when reviewing and consolidating actions, should also review measurement plans to ensure standard methods are used across the entire

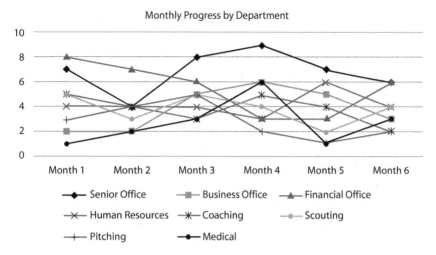

FIGURE 7.2
Honolulu Surfers' Sample Run Chart.

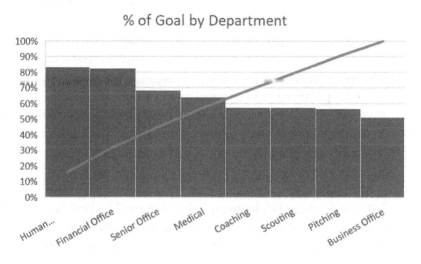

FIGURE 7.3
Honolulu Surfers' Sample Pareto Chart.

organization. This may involve a healthy dose of measurement train-ing for those who are responsible for tracking results. An actual or perceived unfair measurement system could bring down the entire house. Only reliable and fair data should be used for assessment of progress and success.

4. *Problems are visible; therefore, management can place support where needed.* Unfortunately, a typical response to negative trends or performance is to assign blame, followed by a sort of punishment. However, as W. Edward Deming was known for pointing out, "Fear invites wrong figures. Bearers of bad news fare badly. To keep his job, anyone may present to his boss only good news." Deming also believed that in the workplace, there are no bad people, just bad processes. So, rather than assigning blame and punishment to negative findings, perhaps the more logical response is to get help! When a negative trend is identified (and it will be caught early if measurement frequencies are sensitive enough to detect changes), then the best response is to seek the root cause, and address that cause by providing assistance to turn that trend around. What would assistance entail? The answers are endless, e.g., perhaps a process improvement team (the PIT) can be assigned to address the root cause of a failing process, or training for operators might be needed, or better guidance and documentation, or pictures and templates, etc. When the root cause of a problem or negative trend is identified the attendant analysis will provide clues to the necessary corrective action to get back on track to achieve success.

While planning and strategizing are important, the blood, sweat, and tears come into play during deploying and implementing a strategy. The best plans are worthless if they are not implemented. There are many tools available to assist organizations with implementing strategies. Simple examples for documenting details are provided here: Strategy Deployment Table Worksheet (Figure 7.4) and Strategy Deployment Table (Figure 7.5). Both are easy to understand, and can be standardized across the entire organization, allowing for ease in combining and rolling up results for reporting purposes.

In addition, the X-Matrix described in Chapter 5 serves as a visual summary of the organization's strategy, including correlations between Actions and Goals.

Strategy Deployment Table Worksheet

Department:_____

Prepared By:_____

1. Goal or Objective being addressed:

2. Actions to support the Goal or Objective:

3. Tasks and Sub-Tasks (as applicable):

4. Who is responsible for each Action/Task:

5. Timeline to complete the action:

6. How and when the action will be measured:

7. Identify the % complete of each action at each review period.

FIGURE 7.4
Strategy Deployment Table Worksheet.

STRATEGY DEPLOYMENT TABLE

DEPARTMENT:
PREPARED BY:
LAST UPDATED:

GOAL	ACTIONS TO BE TAKEN	TASKS TO SUPPORT ACTIONS	SUB-TASKS	RESPONSIBLE PERSON	DUE DATE	MEASURE-MENT	% COMPLETE

FIGURE 7.5
Strategy Deployment Table.

HONOLULU SURFERS: IMPLEMENTING SPADES STEPS 4–5

We left Chapter 6 with the Honolulu Surfers' organization poised for implementation of the new strategy: Vision, Long-Term Goals, and Short-Term Objectives had been developed and disseminated through the organization and farm teams for feedback. The Owner had personally visited his Honolulu Surfers players and staff, and in an unexpected move, had traveled to the supporting team sites to personally share the Vision with everyone, ensuring that the minor league and farm team players and staff understood the vital role they play in the overall success of the Honolulu Surfers organization.

Vision: World Champions in Paradise

Long-Term Goals:
1. Win the World Series
2. Develop expanded farm clubs in minor leagues
3. Get better connected to our fans

Short-Term Objectives:
1. Win league championship within three years
2. Win our division within two years
3. Win 90+ games within one year
4. Develop minor league affiliates in AAA & AA levels within one year
5. Create local fan-oriented TV show

Two monthly leadership meetings on strategy had taken place and it was time to deploy and implement the new strategy, following SPADES Steps 4 and 5.

SPADES Step 4: Deploy/Roll Down to Departments to Develop Plans

The Honolulu Surfers organization was ready to get moving on the new strategy to drive toward the World Championship. Department leaders and farm team stakeholders were all given the finalized Vision and Goals, along with Strategy Deployment Worksheets and Table templates. While additional notes were allowed, the instructions directed users not to change the formatting of the documents, to allow for ease in rolling up results for reporting purposes. Recommendations for improvement were welcomed and would be considered for future rounds of implementation. Everyone was given a month to work with their staffs to develop the deployment details. Simple instructions were included with the templates:

- Review every Short-Term Objective.
- Assume your department has a role in all Short-Term Objectives, unless proven otherwise.
- Managers develop personal actions along with draft actions for staff.
- Share actions with staff, allowing for feedback and revisions (catchball).
- Conduct a second round of the same.
- Meet with other departments to discuss interactions and dependent activities.
- Finalize all actions, tasks, responsible parties, and due dates.
- Attend "How to Measure your Organization to Achieve Greatness" training on the date announced in separate correspondence.
- Finalize defining measurements to ensure actions are making progress toward goals.
- Send representatives to next month's Honolulu Surfer monthly strategy meeting, with plans to brief deployment tables and details.

The entire organization was put into high speed to accomplish these tasks within a month. The urgency level was intentionally set by top leadership, to make sure everyone understood the importance of the tasking, recognized the priority of deployment as set by the Owner and head staff, and to keep energy levels high.

Field representatives who attended the following Monthly Strategy Meeting were welcomed and treated as important guests. Their messages were met with questions and constructive conversation. It was important for leaders to understand the perspectives of those working with the players and throughout the supporting team structure. A healthy give-and-take took place, and all who attended left the meeting with a much better understanding of the organization's next steps. The Owner was pleased to enter into the implementation phase of the strategy on a very positive note.

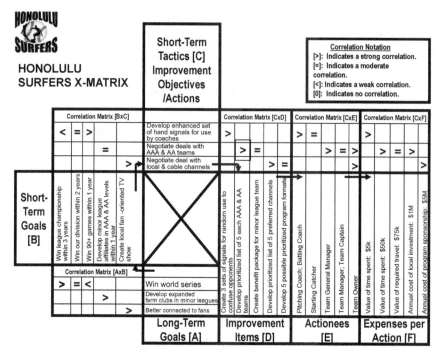

FIGURE 7.6
Honolulu Surfers' X-Matrix.

The SPADES facilitators consolidated input and plans from the organization, confirming linkage to the strategy, using the X-Matrix tool (Figure 7.6).

SPADES Step 5: Implementation

Implementation was like moving into a well-prepared role for the entire organization. Sure, there were a few starts and stops, when a task here or there needed to be adjusted because reality doesn't always match what's planned in a conference room. However, for the most part, implementation went quite smoothly.

Along with the motivational Vision and Goal posters that had popped up on walls, web pages, and letterheads throughout the organization, suddenly visuals lined hallways, showing progress toward the Goals in forms of measurement graphics: although since months one and two were a warming-up period, the Run and Pareto charts that were placed on display showed little new (see Figures 7.7 and 7.8).

No surprise, once everyone realized that performance was displayed for all to see, progress toward completing actions and goals became a healthy competition. No way did the Coaching Staff want to score below the Financial Office! Energy levels were steady and strong.

The first official snag in implementation was hit by the Business Office. Some of the tasks and sub-tasks on their Department Strategy Deployment Table were dependent on other departments. During planning, this wasn't nearly as obvious as when they began to conduct the tasks. Rather

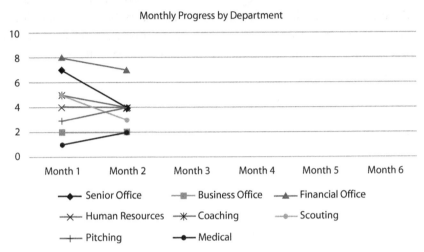

FIGURE 7.7
Honolulu Surfers' Monthly Progress Run Chart.

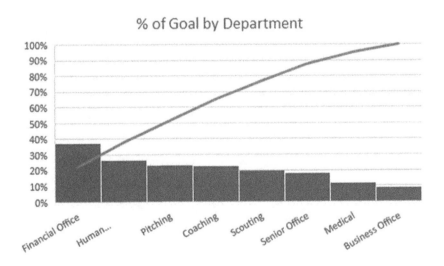

FIGURE 7.8
Honolulu Surfers' Goal Percentage Pareto Chart.

than blame the Business Office for a slow start, the issue was brought up at the following Monthly Strategy Meeting. With all departments represented, a solution was found, and Department Strategy Deployment Tables and Measures were revised. The standard process for identifying, addressing, and solving strategy misalignments was documented and distributed to the entire organization for future issues.

The Honolulu Surfers strategy deployment entered into a steady gear, with every single employee able to quote the organization's vision (World Champions in Paradise), and most able to summarize the Long-Term Goals. Soon, it would be time for official Progress Reviews.... See Chapter 8.

8

Progress and Annual Reviews – SPADES Steps 6–7

The third and final group of SPADES steps is SPADES Steps 6–7: Progress and Annual Reviews. Returning to the ship analogy, when traveling to a distant port, the captain and crew regularly monitor the ship's location, fuel levels, weather, and currents the entire way. These checks are required so as to make necessary course adjustments to ensure they reach their planned destination without disruption. Similarly, once a strategic plan is developed by an organization the deployment and implementation need to be monitored. These regular, periodic reviews need to include analysis of the deployment and implementation metrics established in the prior SPADES steps. This provides the data necessary to develop corrective action plans to adjust for changes in the business environment, personnel, and technology. The frequency of the reviews needs

SPADES Step 1: Establish Organization Vision

SPADES Step 2: Develop Long Term Goals

SPADES Step 3: Develop Short Term and
                Immediate Objectives

SPADES Step 4: Deploy/Roll Down to
                Departments to Develop Plans

SPADES Step 5: Implementation

SPADES Step 6: Progress Review

SPADES Step 7: Annual Review

to support the deployment and implementation milestones, and the length of time and quantity of resources required to develop and execute a recovery plan. Initially, the frequency may be monthly and then adjusted as circumstances dictate.

SPADES STEP 6: PROGRESS REVIEW (MONTHLY AND QUARTERLY)

Recall that during Deployment and Implementation of the Strategic Plan (SPADES Steps 4 and 5), data requirements are defined, and measurement begins. One challenge is determining how many measures are the right amount of measures of performance. Also, where is the best balance point between effort and value when measuring performance? When deploying the strategy was discussed in Chapter 7, all actions were linked to one or just a few key measures. The organization must be able to assess its health and progress. At the same time, don't detract from mission activities by creating measurement tasks that are overburdening to employees. The best measurement system is automatic or not terribly time consuming. It becomes a regular part of daily activities without detracting from the task at hand.

The measures of success include metrics than can be used for a balanced assessment of quality, cost, and schedule. At the operation levels these will be metrics that are counted and/or measured. These measurements are rolled up and, in some instances, transformed into higher-level financial, schedule, and customer satisfaction metrics. Consequently, while each department or office may track several key metrics, perhaps only a subset of those metrics will be of interest to the next level of management for regular reporting purposes. However, when a progress review reveals negative situations, there may be interest in greater breadth of information (counts or measurements), in order to better understand what has gone awry and how to solve the problem and create a recovery plan.

Key Features of SPADES Step 6

The Strategic Plan Actions are now underway. Employees are measuring progress based on agreed upon counts or measures and their frequencies.

There is plenty of activity and information. Now it is time to gather the information to assess progress and performance. What is the right cadence for the organization? Should this take place monthly? Quarterly? Semi-annually? Each organization must make this determination. In the service contracting industry, there are three levels of review frequency: Normal, Increased, and Decreased. When the contract quality is running well, the Normal review frequency is used. When a problem occurs, reviews are adjusted to the increased frequency. And after a long period of good performance, reviews may be reduced to a decreased frequency. The frequencies are set up-front, based on predetermined criteria. Once an original frequency is determined, consider these additional key features of progress reviews:

1. *Strong emphasis on self-diagnosis of targets and process.* Who has the best vantage point to know when something is awry? Who may have first-hand knowledge or ideas on how to improve a situation? If your answer is "employee" or "worker" or something of the sort, we agree. Further, employees must be assessed only for actions within their control. This is not only ideal, it is absolutely necessary. Clear actions and measures create an environment of self-awareness, self-monitoring, and most importantly, self-correcting. Using similar logic as with a service contracting environment, we begin with a level of employee trust. Allow and encourage self-diagnosis and measurement. Only when an employee is proven to be untrustworthy is there a need to move away from this approach. A trusting environment typically results in higher morale, productivity, and retention.

2. *Standardized format and language.* A template that is standard and used by all reduces variance in how progress is reported and assessed. Common language within the template also supports a clearly understood reviewing toolset. By selecting a format, and sticking with it, other than minor adjustments, employees better understand expectations. There are fewer surprises, better reporting results, and more harmony in the workplace.

3. *Simple analysis emphasized.* Complex assessments lead to confusion, and possibly, errors. When assessing progress toward an organization's goals, there is no need to get sidetracked due to overly complicated analyses. Simple is best. This concept blends perfectly with a standard review format and language. Remain clear and concise, simple to perform and simple to understand for employees and employers.

4. *Build plan–do–check–act (PDCA) continuously into process.* Most strategic planning experts are cut from the cloth of performance management and process improvement. The bedrock of our being is based on the scientific method. Any critical decisions require this approach: hypothesis, data selection, data collection, data analysis, and decision; the origin of PDCA. This is the proven methodology for any activity, and it is a must for enacting a strategic plan. The point of SPADES Step 6 is that we have already planned and engaged in tasks, now we are checking the status or results. But checking is not enough. Action must be taken, based on what is found.

5. *Problems are seen as opportunities to be surfaced and resolved, not skeletons to be buried.* In the traditional American auto manufacturing environment, it is a bad thing to stop the production line. Blame and punishment are assigned to anyone who causes a delay in production. During training at the University of Toyota, students were taught to think otherwise. The belief is that if the production line never stops, then mistakes are being missed. Thus, stopping the line is encouraged, and used as an opportunity to improve the production process to prevent future mistakes. This attitude is needed regarding problems in any working environment. There will always be problems, but how much destruction will they cause? That depends on the response. If problems are caught and addressed quickly, the damage is minimized.

6. *Emphasize recognition, support, and corrective action, not punishment.* During the progress review, all outputs can be positive. Clearly when results are above and beyond expectations, recognition is in order. This can take many forms; however, we will not pursue that topic here. But what about the situation where results are not meeting the goal, or data shows a negative trend in performance? Is it time to jump to punishment? Absolutely not! Keep in mind W. Edwards Deming's (the "Father of Quality Management") approach: there are not bad people, just bad processes. Let's help people to succeed. A negative progress review means that someone didn't meet requirements. The next step is to figure out why. Were the necessary tools provided? Did he or she not understand what was required? How can this problem be fixed? How can the person or department be helped to succeed? It is in everyone's best interest to answer these questions.

7. *System problems not directly related to the plan have a place to surface.* This topic is a bit off track, but important. Do the action plans that result from strategic planning touch on everything the company or employee does on a day-to-day basis? Of course not. The strategic plan does directly or indirectly guide the majority of activity. But the standard progress report should include open discussion and documentation of additional problems or opportunities as identified by the employee. Include a location for such a discussion on progress review templates. Don't forget to take advantage of this review time with your greatest resource: your employee. Ask if there are other areas of concern, other ideas that may improve productivity. Document this discussion and make sure these thoughts and ideas are reviewed at the appropriate level of the organization.

8. *Progress reviews are more frequent and less formal that Annual Reviews*, as discussed in the following SPADES step. Why do you think a progress review is needed, if we already intend to hold annual reviews? We could brainstorm a long list of reasons to conduct progress reviews. Here are few thoughts:

   • Progress reviews provide an opportunity to identify and respond to problems much more quickly than annual reviews

   • Progress reviews prevent surprises at the end of the year.

   • Progress reviews uncover issues with employee resources or capability, allowing for resolution in time to meet annual goals.

   • Progress reviews are an opportunity for guidance and adjustment.

   • Progress reviews create an atmosphere of continuous measurement and monitoring.

   • Progress reviews, when done right, increase employee morale and productivity.

SPADES STEP 7: ANNUAL REVIEW

The final SPADES step is the Annual Review. The vision and plan have been developed, long-term goals and short-term objectives are set. All has been disseminated throughout the organization, where mid-level and working-level action plans have been created. Progress reviews have been conducted throughout the year, and now it is time for the big event: The

Annual Review. If all has gone as intended, this will be a highly anticipated event: a chance to bring all the results together to demonstrate how the orchestrated plan has succeeded.

Recall, the organization has developed three- to five-year goals as well as one-year objectives. If the scopes of these targets were appropriate, then the one-year objectives should be met at the time of annual review. Of course, significant progress towards the longer-term goals should be measurable if they are to be of any value to the organization. Returning to the concept of a visual environment, if charts and graphs indicating the current status of the Strategic Plan are placed along hallways or on the opening screen of the company website, then this is a place to display progress.

There may be a few areas that didn't quite reach the planned annual goal. Is this a reason to fret? No, it is time to sharpen pencils and figure out why the target was missed, then plan how to adjust in order to get to the finish line.

Key Features of SPADES Step 7

1. *Data collection and review done all year providing accurate and relevant diagnosis of targets and processes, both good and bad.* A single consolidated dashboard can serve as the visual tool to pull the annual data collection and diagnosis together. This can take the form of a chart or table on the opening screen of a website or primary application. It can also be a whiteboard posted on the shop floor and/or an updatable graphic hanging in the main lobby.

2. *Examine plans even when target is hit, to show correlation.* The emphasis must be on understanding which plans led to achievement of which targets so the resulting process can be standardized. A successful organization learns from both success and failure. In the areas of success, what occurred? How can this successful approach be spread to more organization components? In the areas of failure, what occurred? How can we prevent this from occurring again in the original location as well as in other areas?

3. *Communicate results.* If possible, bring everyone in the organization together using video conference, if available. As with the Vision, the Annual Review is time for everyone to hear with his or her own ears from the very top people in the organization:

Thank you for your hard work. This is where we have succeeded. This is where we need to improve. This is my plan for the next year, and we need you to make it happen. I will do my best to provide you with the resources you need to succeed. Your success is our success.

4. *Celebrate and get ready for an even better year.* The organization, departments, teams, and employees have all worked hard. It's time to celebrate successes. What does this look like? There are endless answers: a company picnic, team lunch or potluck, cake in the break room, company shirts or pens for everyone, a letter of thank you from the owner or Board of Directors, bonuses, etc. Understand your audience and make sure the type of reward (recognition, financial, social, etc.) is valued by your people. Once the celebration is over, teams are rejuvenated and ready to get back to work for an even better next year.

5. *Review the SPADES process itself aiming to improve it for next year.* It's time to return to the Strategic Planning Session group and begin again.

The SPADES seven steps have been designed to provide organization leadership and facilitators with a set of simple guidelines for development of a robust long-term strategy. These steps apply to any organization within any industry. Many tools have been established to assist with strategic planning, however, the roadmap to strategic success has been missing:

SPADES Step 1: Establish Organization Vision
SPADES Step 2: Develop Long-Term Goals
SPADES Step 3: Develop Short-Term and Immediate Objectives
SPADES Step 4: Deploy/Roll Down to Departments to Develop Plans
SPADES Step 5: Implementation
SPADES Step 6: Progress Review
SPADES Step 7: Annual Review

While the Vision and long-term goals from SPADES Steps 1 and 2 are enduring and should not be updated annually, there may be a need from time to time for review and adjustment. Returning to the Strategic Planning Session, it is time to continue the SPADES cycle.

HONOLULU SURFERS: IMPLEMENTING SPADES STEPS 6–7

In Chapter 7, the Honolulu Surfers' set up plans across the entire organization, including minor league and farm teams, with each player informed of what had been planned and engaged with respect to his or her role (several departments were staffed with women including executives). Implementation of the plans had begun, met with a bit of friendly competition across departments, in the quest to meet short-term objectives in support of the long-term goals. A few snags were identified once plans transitioned to actual activities, but those were quickly realized, and then plans were adjusted accordingly.

The entire organization agreed to a frequency of quarterly progress reviews. For the administrative actions, this could simply show continued progress toward the short-term objectives. For the seasonal actions, related to spring training, on- and off-season, this would allow for specific visibility of progress linked to key milestone timing.

First Quarter Performance Review

For most actions and measurements, there were no surprises, because the measurements were tracked real-time, and placed on display at team headquarters, as discussed in the previous chapter (see Figures 8.1 and 8.2):

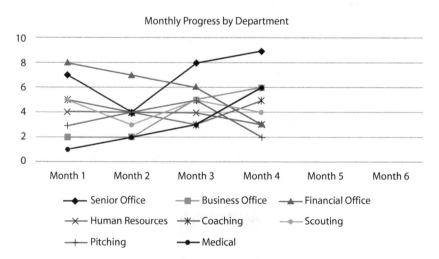

FIGURE 8.1
Honolulu Surfers' 1st Quarter Run Chart.

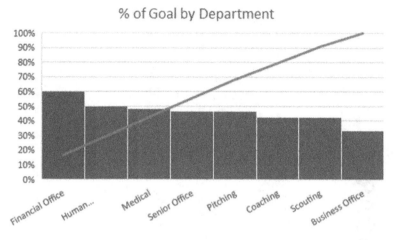

FIGURE 8.2
Honolulu Surfers' 1st Quarter Pareto Chart.

In addition, a dashboard had been created for the internal Honolulu Surfer website, allowing for nearly real-time visibility of the majority of key measurements and progress indicators (see Figure 8.3).

When the standard Action Plan templates were developed, the SPADES facilitators socialized a standard Progress Review template. The standard appearance and features ensured:

- Everyone understood how to complete the forms.
- Measurements could be rolled up to present both a granular and aggregate look at the data.
- Comparisons were equitable and fair.

The first quarter review was treated as a "pilot." Communication was extensive, and everyone from the top managers to local employees knew that the first round of progress reviews would be a period for review and revision as needed. While participants were not allowed to change forms during the review, they were encouraged to provide feedback to the SPADES team, in order to make adjustments prior to the next period of performance and final standardization.

In addition to standard measures, the review templates had an open discussion section allowing for feedback on missed targets, and even issues not listed in the Action Plans. This was an additional opportunity to hear from employees, by requesting their opinions on other problems and opportunities in the organization.

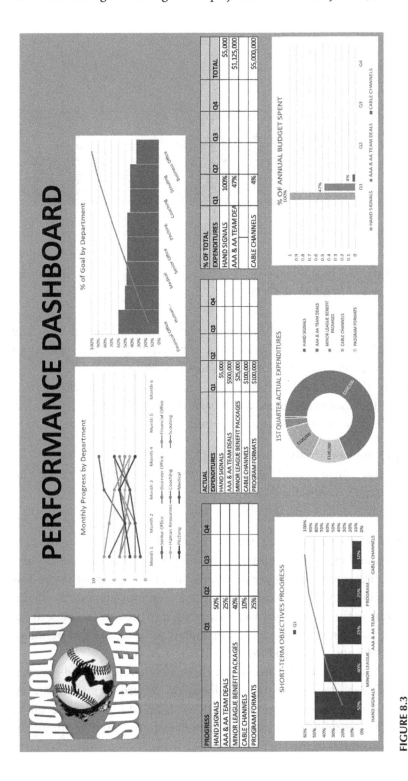

FIGURE 8.3
Honolulu Surfers' Performance Dashboard.

The managers at the major league level, along with the farm system were able to complete the performance review in the requested time period, because the plan in place was a good one, and there was no rush to collect data all at once, since a measurement system of regular accountability was already in place. Instead of a dreaded event, managers were pleasantly surprised to enjoy the opportunity to share their progress and successes with the organization. Employees and managers alike provided nearly unanimous positive feedback.

A recommendation that was quickly acted upon was to create yet another standardized tool: a white board template. All team rooms were already fitted with white boards. It was easy to place standard action tables located in the top right corner of each team room's set of white boards. These action tables had a standard appearance, listing next actions, status, and responsible parties, and due dates. This made the actions easily visible to everyone who entered these rooms.

One of the few "negative" findings during the first quarter review was the rate of spending associated with developing enhanced hand signals for use by the coaches. With 50 percent of the work complete, 100 percent of the budget had been spent. Rather than find someone to blame, the head pitching coach brought the subject matter experts together to figure out the root cause of this discrepancy. It turns out that the mere $5,000 that had been budgeted didn't take into consideration the extent of participants and time needed to develop the quality of hand signals that this group felt was needed. Rather than develop an average signal toolset, the group relayed their desire to raise the bar to develop not only a new group of signals, but a superior set. This would take more time, and more money. After a few follow-up actions, a new budget of $20,000 was agreed to by the experts and pitching coaches. When reflecting on this later, the head pitching coach realized that this was not a negative finding at all. He was pleased to know that the staff took the need for a new signal toolset seriously and didn't plan to settle for anything less than excellent. This was actually a positive event. He made sure to relay it as such during performance reporting.

Annual Performance Review

The standard Progress Review templates were used as the basis for the Annual Review template. With the pilot period complete after first quarter, a few minor adjustments were made and all report formats were finalized.

The first Annual Review with the new Strategic Plan was a huge success! The entire organization eagerly anticipated the opportunity to share results and celebrate together.

The step-by-step planning made it possible for the two primary first-year objectives to be met:

- Win 90+ games
- Develop minor league affiliates at AAA and AA levels.

Honolulu Surfer fans were happy and the base was rapidly growing. The players were bonding as they never had before. The vision of "WORLD CHAMPIONS IN PARADISE" had developed into a real possibility and fans, players, coaches, and managers were excited about their prospects for the future.

At the conclusion of the year, which was also the conclusion of the baseball season, the Owner brought *everyone* together – staff and players from all of the franchise teams – to a resort that was hired out on the island of Maui. After a day of recreation and relaxation, a dinner was held (a luau, of course!) in honor of the entire organization. The Owner took the stage to say a few very important things:

> Thank you for your hard work. This is where we have succeeded [...]. This is where we need to improve. [...] This is my plan for the next year, [...] and we need you to make it happen. I will do my best to provide you with the resources you need to succeed. Your success is our success.

All attendees were given blue and yellow t-shirts sporting the Vision graphic and encouraged to wear the shirts to work on Fridays.

With rejuvenated levels of energy, everyone returned from the working vacation ready for another year of hard work and success.

The Leadership team returned with a clear directive: return to Step 1 and conduct the next annual strategic planning offsite. We will discuss this in the next chapter

9

Reviewing and Refining the Strategy

Yogi Berra once said, "You can observe a lot just by watching." This is what reviewing is all about – observing what is actually happening, being achieved, and the obstacles being encountered. The purpose of a review is to measure progress toward achieving the goals of the plan, evaluate the progress, identify risks to achieving the goals and necessary changes to establish the need for a recovery plan to correct for any variation from the path toward the goals. This is also the point at which leadership may need to adjust goals to accommodate changes in the business environment, technology, and culture.

Review of the strategic plan is all about line of sight from the day-to-day execution of the activities to the operational plan to the strategy. This line of sight provides the opportunity to do the reverse of deployment. Now it can be seen how the various daily and operational plans roll up to achieve the strategy. As the roll-up is conducted, assumptions made in the strategic planning process are tested to see if they are playing out as planned in the operational and daily work of the organization. The review process is a time to adjust the strategic plan if underlying assumptions have changed, competitors have become more aggressive, the marketplace has shifted, customer demands have changed, or the global economy has made a major movement, either positively or negatively.

While strategy review is a continuous improvement process of clarity, the formal review of strategy, possibly conducted via a retreat as described in Chapter 4 or using another method, must be a stand-alone designated working session not to be mixed with scheduled operational reviews. Each organization must develop a strategy review cadence that makes sense for the situation and market. A common frequency is the annual review. The purpose is to "review and renew" the strategy for the organization. A review may result in either slight adjustments, or significant ones, or even no

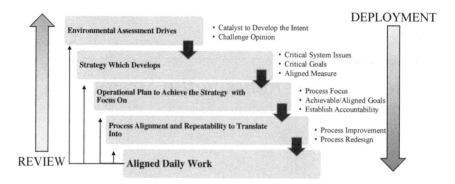

FIGURE 9.1
Goal Deployment and Alignment: Organizational Improvement.

adjustment to the Long-Term Goals and Short-Term Objectives. Most likely Long-Term Goals will remain constant, but if Short-Term Objectives have been met, it will be time to identify the next cycle of work to conduct while seeking to meet the Long-Term Goals.

The strategy review is a time of improvement, learning, and growth for all involved in the review. Figure 9.1, the Goal Deployment and Alignment Model, serves as a reminder of how the strategy deployment and review are linked. Observing this model, it is easy to see that the two have an inverse relationship.

In this chapter, a practical guide for how to run the strategy review is provided. The intent of the review is to provide clarity in the areas of:

- Objectives
- Senior Management's Expectations
- What has been achieved?
- What is on and off course?
- What has not been done?
- What remains to be done?
- Who is responsible to do what and by when?

REVIEW OF PRIOR YEAR (OR OTHER DETERMINED PERIOD) ACCOMPLISHMENTS

A duplicate of the strategy working sessions, previously described in Chapter 4, may be appropriate for this review. However, the initial period of time prior to reviewing and considering adjustments to Goals and Objectives should be dedicated to a review of the prior year's accomplishments. This should be provided by members across multiple layers of the organization. Perhaps higher-level and mid-level managers will be selected to provide this updated information, or select employees who are subject matter experts, representing sections of the organization. Regardless of who is chosen to provide the information, they must have working knowledge of the information being briefed, in order to be able to answer questions that may arise. Some general guidelines for running this portion of the review meeting include:

1. Set the stage for a positive environment and experience. Much like the periodic and annual performance reviews, the intent is not to find problems and affix blame. The intent of the review is to ensure clarity and make appropriate adjustments.
2. As with the initial strategy planning retreat, enlist the expertise of skilled facilitators. With timed briefs and specific outputs needed from the strategy review, it is imperative that third parties run the meeting, allowing participants to focus on content rather than the clock on the wall.
3. Use a simple and standard review slide layout for each Goal or Objective, as shown in Figure 9.2.

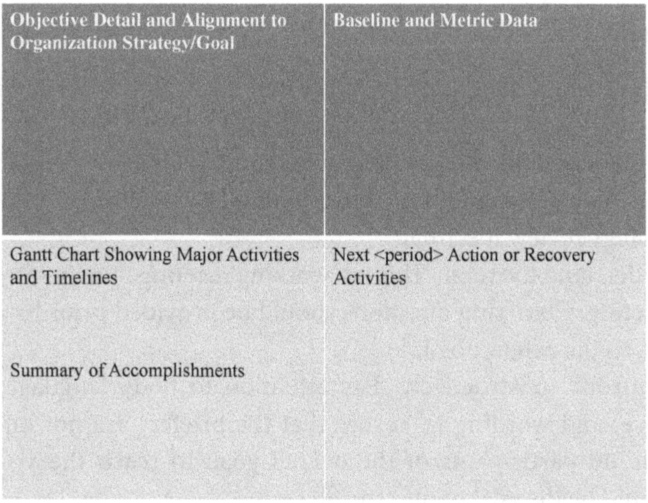

Objective Detail and Alignment to Organization Strategy/Goal	Baseline and Metric Data
Gantt Chart Showing Major Activities and Timelines	Next <period> Action or Recovery Activities
Summary of Accomplishments	

FIGURE 9.2
Review Slide Layout.

4. Establish the expectation that each presentation will be given up to ten minutes. This is not a time for long and detailed presentations. A simple overview will do. Also, it may be necessary to limit the number of slides per presenter. If some background is desired, a limit of three slides during the ten-minute brief is a good guideline.

5. Details are provided in standard review forms and circulated to leadership prior to the review meeting. The standard review forms could be annotated versions of the Strategy Deployment Table and Worksheet described in Chapter 7 (Figures 7.4 and 7.5).

6. Questions should be exchanged in advance, to the greatest extent possible. This goes in both directions: questions for leadership from managers/staff, and questions for managers/staff from leadership. While there will undoubtedly be additional questions at the time of presentation, it is best to share known questions ahead of time to ensure prepared and complete answers.

7. Allow for five minutes of questions and answers at the conclusion of each ten-minute brief.

ROLES AND RESPONSIBILITIES FOR THE REVIEW MEETING

Reviewer

- Follow a standard set of guidelines, such as the Senior Manager Review Checklist provided in Figure 9.3.
- Come prepared. Review progress report information, establish and distribute questions at an agreed period of time prior to the official strategy review meeting.
- Understand the topic. This is a working meeting, not an introductory meeting. Clarifying questions should be provided prior to the meeting, to the extent possible.
- Confront constructively. Pay attention to body language, tone of voice, and wording to ensure that the briefers are not on defense. Remind participants of the overall goal: to reach the vision. This should be the goal of one and all.
- Accept bad news with remedies. Remember that during deployment, a greater understanding of the situation is established. Perhaps what

Senior Management Review Checklist

1. Before The Review:
   a. Familiarize yourself with the Status Reports or Plan/Delta Reports submitted
   b. Inform participants about questions to be asked
   c. Confirm time and place for the Review
   d. Send each participant a completed management review form

2. Before The Review:
   Inform participants about questions to be asked such as:
   a. To which organizational objectives are you aligned?
   b. What are your work unit objectives?
   c. What criteria did you use to choose those objectives/actions?
   d. Who is accountable for objectives being completed?
   e. Why did you choose these improvements?
   f. How will you measure them?
   g. What % completion are you at this point?
   h. Are you on plan or off plan? Why?
   i. Do you have actions detailed to get back on Plan?
   j. What additional resources might you need?
   k. What are the critical processes?
   l. Can these results be replicated elsewhere in the organization?

3. During The Review:
   a. Clarify the purpose of the Review
   b. Stick to the agenda and questions
   c. Look for the alignment of goals and objectives
   d. Ask the agreed upon questions
   e. Create a two-way dialogue and build trust
   f. Probe the goals/objectives/targets - make sure they are stretch
   g. Document agreed upon modifications and follow-up items
   h. Give everyone feedback at the end of the Review
   i. Decide on the time and place of the next Review

4. After The Review:
   a. Send out formal Feedback Report within one week
   b. Document agreements and modifications
   c. Follow-up on agreements
   d. Document obstacles that are common among all teams/participants and start to address them with Executive Level involvement
   e. Prepare notes for next Review

FIGURE 9.3
Senior Manager Review Checklist.

was planned in a conference room didn't reflect reality. If an objective was not met, or a goal is identified as not the best goal, then treat it as the boost in knowledge that it is. The information is helpful in refining the next steps and strategy.

- Probe for specifics. When generalities are used, this could cover problem areas or subjects that are uncomfortable for the briefer. Painting over a blemish using a broad and often positive statement is a common human behavior. Ask questions for clarity so as to minimize misunderstandings.
- Look for alignment between status, activities, objectives, and goals. In addition, treat each briefer not only as an individual but as a member of the whole. Continue to consider the big picture while listening to details of each piece being briefed.
- Challenge where appropriate. When done well, this inspires and energizes members of the organization. People long to feel as though they are contributing and making an important difference. Encourage them to do so. If a goal is met on time or ahead of schedule, ask the presenter for his or her opinion of how to reach further for a greater result. If a goal is not met, figure out why and challenge the organization to correct and establish a goal that is a better fit for the situation. Place this in the context of reaching the vision. Always return to the vision.

Reviewee

- Come prepared. Be familiar with progress report information and have answers to management questions that were distributed prior to the review meeting. If detailed inquiries are expected, bring one or two topical experts along to help answer questions.
- Have "Why's" ready. Be prepared to discuss root causes and potential solutions to issues and findings from the past year of activities.
- Action plans to convert deltas. Where an objective was not met, or was met in advance of plans, discuss the reasons for any changes from plans. Make recommendations in response to the changes.
- Show alignment to organizational objectives. This is important. In order to prevent "silo thinking," make sure that not only this strategy review meeting, but also periodic progress reviews keep the big picture in mind. How are the local activities and objectives linked to the organization as a whole as well as to other parts of the organization?

- Discuss bad news. Don't skim over the negative news. This is the area where managers may be able to help the most. If an objective was not met, discuss why. Was more training needed, or more resources? Was there a process issue preventing the necessary progress? This is a chance to get the ear of the person who can remove roadblocks and help clear the way for success. Treat it as a very important opportunity.
- Accept challenges. Good managers will ask the hard questions, and the responses need to be truthful, yet open-minded. Is there a way to do more with less? Can processes continue to improve? Was an objective from the prior year too easy to reach? How can your team contribute even more towards reaching the organizations vision and goals?
- Be accountable. This is not just about accepting responsibility. This is about having the data to back up what is being discussed. As mentioned previously, opinions are good – and they are often correct, but data is the only way to prove it. Make sure that what is being reported includes quantitative data to back it up.
- Expect adjustments. The entire reason for a strategy review is to validate and adjust the prior period strategy. Based on the communications shared during the strategy review followed by leadership digestion and understanding, changes will come next. Don't blow your chance to engage and shape these changes, make sure to participate wholeheartedly in order to create an environment for the best possible adjustments and results.

REFINE THE STRATEGY

The Strategy of an organization is an enduring document and journey. Most likely, there will not be significant changes from year to year. However, given another year of information and maturity, the need for adjustments to the strategy may reveal itself. This is exactly where the organization is, following the annual review: a fork in the road. Notice, the tines of the fork continue in the same general direction, but each one is just slightly off by a few degrees. Are refinements needed? The answer to that question will be fairly clear, if the review described in this chapter is thorough and if those who provide the information have been forthcoming and honest.

Following the review, top leadership (Senior and Executive Leaders) should have some thoughts on modifications to the strategy. Strike while the iron is hot. This is not a time to return to the office with a meeting scheduled for weeks or a month in the future. While thoughts are fresh, it is time to discuss any impressions and needs for modifications to the plan. A facilitated session the day of the review briefings or the following day is the best timing for such a discussion. Sure, there may be the need to ask a few more questions of the presenters or collect some clarifying data, but that can be done post haste.

Within a week of the formal review, documentation of modifications should be disseminated through the organization for feedback. This should sound familiar. Reviewing and refining the strategy is simply returning to the beginning of SPADES, and conducting the next cycle. Return to Chapters 3 and 4, to recall what happens next.

HONOLULU SURFERS: REVIEWING AND REFINING STRATEGY

Recall that in Chapter 8 the progress and annual reviews took place to determine the status of actions and objectives for the Honolulu Surfers' organization. The advancement toward Goals and the ultimate vision of winning the World Series were measured and reported. The year concluded with a grand celebration, and a renewed energy level for all.

As with any strategy it was then time to not only review progress, but to circle back to review the strategy itself. With year one in the rearview mirror, the organization had a fresh and realistic perspective on the vision and goals set at the beginning of the prior year.

The Owner and top managers met to discuss how to proceed. The answer was fairly obvious: begin the year again with a retreat. This year, instead starting from scratch, they would start with some experience, which would serve as a great advantage! In addition to using the tools discussed in Chapter 3, the Current State assessment, determining Customer Needs and Wants, and refining the Future State estimate, they now had the year both in counts and measurements as well as feedback from players, subject matter experts, and managers across the entire organization to benefit the strategy planning.

The Managers agreed to a slightly revised retreat agenda. This time, they would invite representatives from across the organization to participate for the first part of the retreat. They would use this rich source of information to set the stage for the strategy review. A standard briefing template was developed to summarize progress during the first year, along with recommendations for following years. Questions from the Owner and the Managers were consolidated and disseminated to the teams and staffs for consideration. A responding set of questions was documented through the team website and consolidated for manager consideration prior to the retreat.

The SPADES facilitators were assigned the administrative role for consolidating and preparing not only content and agenda, but also retreat logistics.

Last year, the Owner hosted the strategy planning at his home. It was a lovely venue, but given the increased number in attendance this year, it wouldn't do. So, a site was selected near the North Shore, with overnight accommodations and meals included. The Owner felt that a beautiful and open physical environment would help to create a positive working environment for all in attendance.

As was his way, the Owner opened the event with a surprise. He had asked the team MVP from the prior season to kick off the retreat, with a heart-felt speech from his perspective about the changes in the organization. The MVP talked about "these posters that started showing up around the hallways," and discussions of something called a "vision." He described that at first the players thought it was a joke. They kidded around about it. But, as they encountered their support staff and coaches, and realized that this was being taken seriously, their opinions began to change. The serious planning and intentional changes that went into the back-meeting rooms and farm teams created a level of intensity that grew through spring training and into the regular season. The players felt supported as never before and the quality of coaching and pitching improved noticeably. It seemed that everyone grew closer together, including the dedicated fans. Something that began as just another management instrument turned into a real live wave of growth for the entire organization. He and his teammates discussed it and were astounded to see how they were personally affected. He thanked the Owner and everyone in attendance for their hard work, which made the players' hard work turn into better results than they could have expected. Rather than dreading any future changes, he was looking forward to them, because he trusted this group and had seen last year what they could do for the Honolulu Surfers' organization.

What a way to start the retreat! It's not always easy for someone in an administrative role to see how he or she directly benefits a player, but this speech made it personal for everyone in attendance. The MVP's speech was recorded, in order to disseminate it along with the strategy revisions to the entire organization for year-two deployment.

Next, the short briefings began. Managers and representatives from across the entire organization were each introduced and given ten minutes to provide an overview of the prior year from their perspectives in relation to the organization's strategy. By using the standard briefing template, and answering predocumented questions, it was easy to stay on track. While brief, the content was purposeful and truthful. Areas of difficulty from the prior year, as discussed in Chapter 8, were highlighted along with successes. The managers and representatives shared thoughts and ideas along with their briefs. The SPADES facilitators kept a running list of issues and recommendations as they were brought up by briefers and the audience. By the time the fifteenth, and final, briefer finished, the morning had all but flown by.

At lunch, the Owner took the microphone and welcomed an assorted group of people who stood behind him. It turns out he had invited a small group of fans to join them for the hour, offering an opportunity to share from their perspectives what had happened over the prior season. A man and his son of about ten years spoke first. They were thrilled about the extra wins over prior years. An older woman talked about the pitching and how the new team closer made the games more exciting. Another fan discussed how he would like to have the opportunity to watch more games and interviews on-line. Several mentioned that they felt the team was working toward a real shot at the World Series. One man hoped that ticket prices wouldn't increase with the new success – it was all he could do now to afford season tickets. Hearing feedback directly from the fans meant a lot to the planners at the retreat. They would have those faces and voices in mind as they worked to review and revise the organization's strategy.

After lunch, some of the morning briefers along with the fans departed. It was time for those who remained to roll up their sleeves, ready to begin working with the same agenda used the prior year. This time, starting from a new level, with the past year behind, a great deal more knowledge, and some momentum toward the vision. They were warmed up and ready to play.

(What did they do next? Go back to Chapter 3 to review the Honolulu Surfers scenario. Round 2 of the strategy planning session ensued.)

10

Organizational Challenges and Cures

The introduction of anything new or unique is accompanied by challenges to its implementation. The success of SPADES depends on identifying and managing challenges to the process. The challenges will include resistance and will be manifested as problems presented by those who want to maintain the status quo or by the manner in which it is implemented. Some of these problems can be avoided by careful preparation. Others will require corrective action and recovery planning to stay the course to the strategic goals. This chapter presents the common challenges experienced, during a period of change, with associated corrective or preventive actions. Note these challenges apply to any other new or unique process or method that may be introduced to an organization, e.g., quality management, safety practices, or environmental concerns.

The organizational challenges are organized into four categories, i.e., Strategy, Leadership, Personnel, and Data. Strategy is the "process" and its implementation. Leadership refers to the communication, delegation, and follow-through required to organize and motivate personnel to accomplish the deployment and implementation of the "process." Personnel encompasses the complete workforce of the organization which carries out the tasks and responsibilities for execution of the "process" defined by the leaders. Data refers to the metrics that are collected for measuring progress.

The challenges that may be encountered in SPADES are described in the following paragraphs. The tables present the Challenges with recommended Preventive Actions and Cures.

1 STRATEGY

1.1 Lack of Strategic Focus

This is a lack of a common understanding of the purpose and goals for the organization and/or a clear understanding of the purpose of the strategic planning session among the key members of the leadership team and strategic planning support personnel. Engineering, Manufacturing, Human Resources, Finance, and so on have a significant role in achieving the mission of the organization. Their participation in SPADES is critical for success of the strategic planning of the organization. Each person brings a focus based on the reference of their individual experiences, knowledge, and responsibilities. In order to ensure all have a common understanding of the goals of SPADES and are working together for the same goals it is critical that all members of the organization responsible for the development of the strategy and its implementation have a clear and complete understanding of their role and responsibilities for the strategic planning and implementation.

1.2 SPADES Process Not Followed Methodically

This obstacle is simply a result of human nature. We are built to solve problems. We naturally rush to solutions. When strategic planning is not conducted in a methodical way, from broad plans to specific plans, a forced-fit is the result. The employees or management document actions or goals and back into objectives, or actions are tacked onto deployment plans without clear connection to broader, long-term content.

1.3 Strategic Planning Becomes a Science Project

This obstacle is insidious. This often occurs when the "satisfaction" of the act of analysis and planning overshadows the importance of results. It is, in fact, when the purpose of strategic planning is to make a plan and not to achieve the vision and goals of the organization.

Strategic planning is critical to the success of the organization. It needs, however, to be rigorous and timely. It is a serious function but it requires a level of importance and urgency so it doesn't become a never-ending science project or social event.

TABLE 10.1

Strategy Challenges

Which cure needs to be applied when SPADES implementation encounters the following Strategy Challenges?	Preventive Actions and Cures
1.1 Lack of Strategic Focus This occurs when there is a lack of common understanding and agreement of the purpose and goals for the organization and/or a clear understanding of the purpose of the strategic planning session among the key members of the leadership team and strategic planning support personnel.	Written statements of purpose, goals, and objectives facilitates a common understanding. Furthermore, open discussions and consensus decision making facilitate ownership of the plan and thereby create support by all the participants.
1.2 SPADES Process not followed methodically When strategic planning is not conducted in a methodical way, from broad plans to specific plans, a forced-fit deployment of plans without clear connection to broader, long-term content.	The solution to this challenge is to engage experienced facilitators during the strategy planning sessions. Diligently follow the SPADES steps to develop a sound and solid plan. Use the "catchball" approach (see Chapter 7) for deployment and implementation planning.
1.3 Strategic Planning Becomes a Science Project This is when the purpose of strategic planning is to make a plan and not to achieve the vision and goals of the organization.	This challenge to SPADES can be prevented or resolved through rigorous planning, identification of accountability for action, documented scheduling, and regular periodic reviews followed by recovery plans as necessary. Recovery plans need assigned accountability, specific deliverables and firm scheduled completion dates.
1.4 Strategic Planning Becomes Stagnant and the Process Becomes Intransigent The structure and execution of the planning process does not provide for rapidly detecting and adapting to new techniques, concepts, or information.	Documented SPADES plans of action with assigned responsibility, firm performance schedules with defined regular, periodic reviews will prevent or cure this challenge. The frequency of the reviews needs to be aligned with the deployment schedule to provide early identification of this challenge. In the absence of these steps they will need to be implemented when the SPADES execution meets this challenge.

1.4 Strategic Planning Becomes Stagnant and the Process Becomes Intransigent

Strategic planning is critical to the success of the organization. It needs, however, to be rigorous and timely. It is a serious function but it requires a high level of importance and urgency so it doesn't become a never-ending science project or social event.

This challenge to successful SPADES occurs when the structure and execution of the planning process does not provide for rapidly detecting and adapting to new techniques, concepts or information.

Honolulu Surfers: Strategy Challenges

Even though the Honolulu Surfers were new to the concept of strategic planning using the SPADES approach, the Owner and top managers were fortunate to have hired facilitators with a clear understanding of the importance of avoiding Strategy Challenges. The approach used was focused and methodical from the pre-planning and the initial strategic planning retreat, to deployment, and monitoring of progress. The Surfers were able to evade common missteps because of the quality of preparation and use of experienced support. There were a few problems that surfaced along the way, but not due to strategy, but rather due to other organizational challenges as discussed below.

2 LEADERSHIP

2.1 Unrealistic Vision, Mission, Goals or Objectives

This obstacle occurs when the vision, strategy, goals, objectives, or plans are not achievable. Perhaps during the strategy planning session, the participants become excited and in a state of exhilaration begin to reach for the stars. This can be a good thing, within reason. But, if the output from leadership reaches the workers and they realize that next year's goals are well beyond reasonable, it can have a deflating effect. Imagine beginning the year with an expectation that at the end of the year you will stand to be judged on something that is out of your control. I think it would be time to look for other employment.

2.2 Incorrect Focus

This obstacle occurs when the majority of focus is the wrong thing. As an example, let's say an organization has significant financial audit issues. The next year, in an effort to improve, the organization's vision is adjusted to address solid financial controls. The strategy then circles the wagons around creating the best, most solid financial internal controls known to man. All supporting documentation is aligned with the internal control focus. Inspections and measures document the quantity and adherence to controls and quality checks. The organization has great success with their controls. However, the next year finds that the financial reporting is still experiencing discrepancies. What happened? The controls were in place and being met.

The problem was the wrong focus. Fix the issue, then monitor and control results. The financial tools themselves were not addressed, although you can argue that their shortcomings could have become evident via the newly established controls. This is akin to standardizing a bad process. While standardizing is good, the process must first be worthy of standardizing.

2.3 Disingenuous Participation by Leadership

The flip side of the coin from Problem 2.1 is fake participation by leadership. This obstacle happens when leaders know they need to complete a strategic plan. They have a facilitator to help them develop the key elements of the plan. They use the right word, and come up with a reasonable product, but don't believe or don't plan to really live a word of it.

Employees, indeed most humans, can sense insincerity. It is almost better to forgo any planning than to develop an inspiring strategic plan and not follow through with deploying the plan. Worse is an organization with low employee morale that develops a list of principles where employees are stated to be important to the organization, while in reality they are treated poorly. This causes a rift between workers and management. It causes discontent and results in distrust.

2.4 Lack of Clear Guidance

This obstacle occurs during deployment of the strategy. If top-level guidance isn't clear, facilitators are not available, catchball or some feedback loops are not used, then it is an easy transition for mid-level engagement to twist the original intent of the strategy to something that reflects the drive of local managers. This change in direction can make it very difficult to reach goals and objectives, and nearly impossible to ever experience the vision of the organization.

2.5 Repetition Expecting Different Results

In a recent strategy meeting, one of the participants stated that we were in "Back to the Future." He further explained that everything that was being discussed had already been discussed during previous years. And we found ourselves in the same place yet again. This obstacle can occur for many reasons: an unproductive prior year strategy, changes in personnel without retention of organizational knowledge, or perhaps lethargy.

2.6 Deployment is Stalled

If deployment of the strategy does not produce results, something is wrong. A complete strategy that doesn't drive the organization forward may mean there is a leadership issue: the sailboat has been built, everyone is on board, but there is no movement.

2.7 Ineffective Review Process

The words "performance review" in most organizations equate to fear, i.e., fear of punishment for results not achieved. Performance reviews are usually unpleasant experiences. Think of the many reviews you may have been subjected to over the years. The annual medical review, a tax review, a performance review, a fitness for duty review, a mid-term school review, and so on. All of us had some level of fear in each one of them since we knew something would be said or discovered that would indicate we were headed for trouble or a discomforting experience. What we feared in these reviews as individual participants was reprisal for certain actions taken or not taken. Usually, the reviewer, whether senior, middle- or first-line manager, does not find the review process any more pleasant than the reviewee since they seem to chastise all too often and seldom take the time to recognize achievements.

2.8 Rewards and Recognition Not Commensurate with Accomplishments

This issue occurs when people are rewarded too soon, or for minimal results. The time has passed for length of service to be a primary determinant for compensation and bonuses. These days we have the tools to measure performance, and the expectation is that people will be rewarded for performance (or the opposite). This can be applied to execution of a strategy as well.

Honolulu Surfers: Leadership Challenges

Once deployment began for the Surfers' strategy, there were a few bumps in the road. This was a new way of thinking, a new approach for many of the mid-level management staff. Pitching coaches had never been held to direct account for progress due to hand-signals and pitching staff; affiliate teams were new and trying to understand how they would support the overall Honolulu Surfers strategy. The Owner received feedback that some in the middle were less than enthusiastic. As mentioned in Challenge 2.3 above, they were somewhat disingenuous. Perhaps they thought that this management interest would come and go, as many do. But, once the Owner was aware of the situation, he decided to personally address it. He scheduled official meetings with the pitching coaches, and affiliate managers. He assured them that he was "all-in" with the vision of becoming World Champions, and the road that had been developed to reach that vision. He also made unplanned visits to assure staff that he was interested in their progress even between official updates. He was genuine and wanted their feedback. He wanted to understand the everyday challenges and attitudes toward the organization's strategy. Due to

TABLE 10.2

Leadership Challenges

Which cure needs to be applied when SPADES implementation encounters the following Leadership Challenges?	Preventive Actions and Cures
2.1 Unrealistic Vision, Mission, Goals or Objectives This is when the vision, strategy, goals, objectives, or plans are not achievable.	This challenge to successful SPADES is often the result of group think or ineffective facilitation. Strategic planning needs to create a sense of excitement and enthusiasm, and renewed commitment to success and growth. The vision, associated mission, and the supporting goals all need to be specific, achievable, and relevant. The regular, periodic Review Process will facilitate the prevention of this challenge. It will also provide an insight into areas of the vision, mission, and goals that may need to be adjusted.
2.2 Incorrect Focus This challenge occurs when the majority of focus is on the wrong vision, mission, or goals. This is akin to standardizing a bad process.	If the first-year actions and measures don't produce desired results, it is time to take the lessons learned, adjust the focus, and return with a better plan.
2.3 Disingenuous Participation by Leadership This challenge is fake participation by leadership. Leaders know they need to accomplish. They use the right words. They may develop a reasonable deliverable, but don't believe in it nor do they plan to implement the plan.	The simple cure is sincerity. When documenting the Mission, Vision, Goals, or Values the words need to be true. Leaders need to recognize past problems, acknowledge and state the problems to the workforce, and sincerely communicate a desire to fix past wrongs.
2.4 Lack of Clear Guidance This challenge occurs during deployment of the strategy. If top level guidance isn't clear, it is easy for mid-level leaders to twist the original intent of the strategy thereby making it difficult to reach goals and objectives.	Communication, feedback, facilitation, and monitoring of deployment are necessary to avoid or respond when this challenge occurs. Once high-level leaders pass their plans to the next levels for action, they need to remain engaged and actively involved throughout the year. Without continued leadership engagement, the rest of the organization will perceive SPADES is no longer important "at the top," and the momentum will be lost, resulting in failure.

2.5 Repetition Expecting Different Results

This challenge is when action is taken that doesn't yield the desired results, and then the same action is repeated, without changes in approach.

A solid and productive strategy may normally experience slow progress. If there is zero growth this may be the result of going back to the future, again and again, i.e., repeating actions again and again and expecting different results. The cure for this challenge begins with a cause and effect analysis to determine the reasons for this stagnation. The analysis may indicate a need for refresher SPADES training, engaging new facilitators, adjusting roles and responsibilities, or revamping the measurement system.

2.6 Deployment is Stalled

Deployment of the strategy does not produce results.

The first response to this challenge needs to be renewed leadership engagement. This may mean cranking up the volume to an entirely different level. Instead of an annual town hall, perhaps the "big boss" needs to walk around and talk to individuals. Maybe it's time for a company-wide stand-down for an afternoon where team building takes place and the leaders engage directly with all employees to emphasize the importance of the strategy and plans in support of the strategy. A renewed emphasis on measures, while linking annual performance appraisals and bonuses to documented results can be used to move the boat.

2.7 Ineffective Review Process

Regular, periodic reviews of plans of actions and milestones, as well as measurements and analysis of progress toward goals and objectives are critical to success in SPADES as it is in any project or task. This challenge is when the review process does not produce accurate and timely information to evaluate the execution of SPADES and develop appropriate recovery plans.

The purpose of a review is to develop mutual understanding among leadership and process owners about objectives, goals, actions, alignment, and timing. In addition, the review process needs to provide accurate, progress measurements. It is critical the timeliness of the measurements provides sufficient time to develop and execute corrective action plans in order to keep SPADES on track. If it is determined the review process is inadequate, it needs to be re-engineered to ensure accurate and timely measurements of progress.

2.8 Rewards and Recognition Not Commensurate with Accomplishments

This challenge occurs when people are rewarded too soon, or for minimal results.

SPADES is about results not action. While it is important to recognize the accomplishment of milestones, it's important to hold the big celebrations for big achievements. A plan to do something is NOT a big achievement. Enacting the plan and reaching performance targets or exceeding goals are worthy of celebration. Equally rewarding progress or small accomplishments and big accomplishments diminishes the importance of all accomplishments.

this time invested in visits, communication, and consistency, the "frozen middle" did thaw, and those who weren't first to jump on the SPADES bandwagon eventually aligned to the plan.

---

3 PERSONNEL

3.1 False Employee Engagement

This challenge creates long-term mistrust across the organization. It occurs when Leadership shares the plan and asks for employee engagement, but then doesn't provide any proof that the input from others was considered.

Strategic Planning at its core requires buy-in from the entire organization. By appearing to request input but then not considering or showing changes based on input, or minus feedback to the organization, people begin to feel jaded and cheated. They may outwardly appear to support the entire strategic planning effort, but internally feel cheated or deceived.

3.2 Storming

The four phases of group development are known to be Forming, Storming, Norming, and Performing. It is a natural tendency for groups (or individuals) who come together for a new purpose to initially experience positive feelings and excitement, followed by a reality check and then possibly a deflation of enthusiasm or even group discord. The important thing to remember is that this is normal. So normal, in fact, that this four-phase model was developed and has been commonly referred to for over 50 years.

3.3 Warring Factions

Some people enjoy a battle, or haggling, or a well-fought negotiation. They have a natural tendency to argue or state a contrary opinion. This personality trait may expose itself during strategic planning. If not managed, it can get out of hand, creating long-term angst or memory of hurt feelings. What's worse is that bad actors can take advantage of this type of situation and build alliances that go against harmony and loyalty. A 1954 classic children's fairy tale by Dr. Seuss, "Horton Hears a Who!", had an appropriate quote for the results of this process: "I'm an elephant and elephants never forget, it's a curse really!"

3.4 Inflexibility

This obstacle occurs when too much emphasis is placed on the longevity of the vision and plan. Leaders become inflexible because they think they must stick with long-term goals as originally written.

3.5 Saboteurs

We have all seen this in one form or another. This is the "water cooler person" who is all smiles and nods in the planning meetings, but once out in the hallway, next to the water cooler, the truth of his or her feelings are shared. This person may privately or publicly declare that the plan is hogwash and he or she has no intention of supporting it. Depending on the circle of influence held by this person, actions contrary to the intent of the plan may begin to take place by one or more people. Heaven help us if this person is a mid-level manager. The frozen middle may become a reality, with no communication or clear direction making it to the working level in that section of the organization.

Honolulu Surfers: Personnel Challenges

In addition to some of the roadblocks experienced by middle management, there was a bit of "storming" across the organization during the first year of deploying the strategy. The Honolulu Surfers was a somewhat successful organization prior to SPADES, but attempting to win the World Series in a matter of five years? That seemed a stretch or pipe dream to many of the staff members and even some players. As commonly experienced by teams of all kinds, the Surfers' organization

TABLE 10.3

Personnel Challenges

Which cure needs to be applied when SPADES implementation encounters the following Personnel Challenges?	Preventive Actions and Cures
3.1 False Employee Engagement This challenge occurs when employees outwardly appear to support the entire strategic planning effort, but internally don't believe in it.	The successful implementation of SPADES requires a clear and communicated feedback loop that addresses incoming content across all levels of the organization. Even if a recommendation is not incorporated into the final product, as long as sound explanation is given as to why, employees will feel that their voices have been heard, and will not automatically shut off their support for the endeavor.
3.2 Storming This challenge is one of the four phases of group development known as Forming, Storming, Norming, and Performing. Storming is the tendency for groups (or individuals) who have come together for a new purpose to initially experience positive feelings and excitement which is then followed by a level of deflation of enthusiasm and/or group discord.	Perhaps the best way to address storming during the strategy implementation is to explain the Teaming Process. Explain Storming was to be expected. And then describe the additional phases to come: Norming and Performing. It's also important to understand changing any aspect of the Performing group may create another cycle of Forming, Storming, Norming, and Performing to come.
3.3 Warring Factions This challenge involves individuals who have a tendency to argue and be negative. In extreme instances these individuals may build alliances that work against the process.	It's important to recognize this challenge early. When negativity becomes vocal during strategy planning sessions, or if groups begin to align against each other, it is time to break up the action. Stop the work. Reconvene at a later date. Address people privately to get to the root causes of the disagreements and discuss ways to resolve issues before returning to the strategy sessions. Build trust with participants who can then believe that their interests and opinions will have a role in the process. The offender or manipulator may need to be dealt with separately. It's important that people understand and believe that the purpose of strategic planning is to increase the organization's successes, which ultimately benefit all: employees and customers.

3.4 Inflexibility

This challenge involves over-emphasizing the longevity of the vision and plan. Leaders become inflexible because they think they must stick with long-term goals as originally written.

Successful strategic planning requires organizational growth, learning, and adjustments for changing technology and environments. It will take time before an organization reaches the sweet spot of SPADES truly guiding the organization as intended. It is critical that leadership understands this and communicates it to the personnel. Leaders need to ensure all embrace the idea it is okay to make rudder changes along the way. And in fact, is expected and is encouraged.

3.5 Saboteurs

This challenge includes the individuals who are all smiles and nods in the planning meetings, but once out in the hallway privately or publicly declare disapproval of the plan. They also work against the implementation of SPADES.

This challenge will become evident during the deployment phase of SPADES. Progress reviews and deployment metrics will show negative results, delayed reporting or ball-parking, and fudging may become the modus operandi of these individuals. A comprehensive deployment plan requiring measured results with regular periodic progress reviews spotlight on this problem and the saboteurs. Saboteurs need to be addressed. If they refuse to join the "team" that is the organization, they need to be fired.

members, particularly those who were engaged from the very first planning retreat, initially found the can-do spirit, and excitement, even positive electricity, that went along with beginning a new journey toward a lofty vision. But within weeks, as the drive of daily progress toward the vision took its toll and the new challenge of monitoring progress took hold, the storming phase was inevitably entered.

Rather than throw in the towel, agree that this was simply too hard, and the organization was too young to achieve the vision of a world championship, the Owner and top managers sought out the advice of their SPADES facilitators. These experts had extensive experience with teams and the phases of group development. They assured the Owner and managers that this was a normal part of the process, and not to be too alarmed, and certainly not to be derailed by the negativity that accompanies a storming phase. As a matter of fact, entering the storming phase is proof of progress, the people who need to get the work done are understanding that it will be a challenge, a difficult road. Beyond storming, they could look forward to the cohesiveness that would come with norming and then the successes associated with performing. The facilitators asked the Owner to recall any team he had been a part of through life – had they experienced forming, storming, norming, and performing? And by golly, he realized they had!

A light bulb turned on, and the Owner developed a summary of a personal experience he had during an earlier time in his life. He decided to go on the road, to talk with the Surfers' staff, players, and affiliate teams to share this story. He assured them that storming was a normal part of any successful team model. Rather than assume that storming was the end of the road, realize that it was proof of true team development and a step toward success. This road trip was well worth the time, helping to ease many concerns, and further develop comradery across the entire organization.

4 DATA

4.1 Lack of Timely, Relevant, or Accurate Data

The goal for strategic planning is to develop a clear and accurate understanding of the values and purpose of the organization and to develop a fact-based plan for achieving the goals that support the purpose of the organization. Fact-based decisions, by definition, depend on timely, relevant, and accurate data. Problems generated by this Challenge exist when data used in the SPADES process is inaccurate, irrelevant, insufficient, or out of date. When this problem occurs, it dooms the strategic plan and the organization to failure.

4.2 Insufficient Attention to Detail

This obstacle is when the accuracy and completeness of each step does not meet the requirements of the planning process. There are many parts to this obstacle to success. It may be not having all the appropriate stakeholders involved in SPADES, lack of rigorous accomplishment of each step of the process, or lack of understanding of the accuracy of data collected.

4.3 Metrics are Not Useful for Evaluating Progress

Even if all of the words are correct and beautifully written with respect to goals, objectives, and action plans, if the measures are off, we are sunk. As we all know, measurements affect behavior. The wrong metrics can drive the organization onto an unwanted path. If we are too focused on what may be traditional measures of the organization (such as efficiencies of individual sections, or obligation rates regardless of results or value), without re-evaluating those measures to make sure they drive behaviors toward needed actions, then the entire strategy planning exercise may be a waste of time.

4.4 Form Over Substance

It's easy these days to find people who are skilled in the art of flashy marketing tools. This obstacle is a result of producing beautiful, shiny signs, colorful booklets, the loveliest of mugs that all reflect a shell of a strategy without much meat or content. Remember the Wendy's commercials from decades ago: "Where's the beef?"

TABLE 10.4

Data Challenges

Which cure needs to be applied when SPADES implementation encounters the following Data Challenges?	Preventive Actions and Cures
4.1 Lack of Timely, Relevant or Accurate Data Fact-based decisions, by definition, depend on timely, relevant, and accurate data. Problems generated by this Challenge exist when data used in the SPADES process is inaccurate, irrelevant, insufficient, or out of date.	This challenge can be prevented or corrected by written requirements for the data to be collected and its purpose. When data is collected it is critical that the data collection method, data source, and accuracy are documented. This will enable the decision makers to know and understand how the data supports their decisions and how much they can rely on the data in making fact-based decisions.
4.2 Insufficient Attention to Detail This challenge occurs when the accuracy and completeness of each step does not meet the requirements of the planning process.	Strategic planning needs to be a core business process. Each step of SPADES needs to be thoroughly executed. Progress and results need to be timely and accurate. This requires data accuracy requirements to be documented and understood by the participants in the SPADES process. This will ensure decisions are fact-based and leaders will understand the reliability of their decisions.
4.3 Metrics are not useful for evaluating progress This challenge occurs when measurements are not accurate, frequency of measurement is inadequate for timely evaluation of the progress, or metrics are inappropriate for evaluating progress.	This challenge can be prevented by establishing a comprehensive measurement, analysis, and reporting process. It is recommended an experienced process analyst assists in establishing process metrics and measurement systems and guiding analysis. Train employees to understand this critical tool for monitoring and controlling results. When measurements don't provide the intended information, adjust measurement process.
4.4 Form over substance This challenge is a result of producing beautiful, shiny signs, colorful booklets, the loveliest of mugs that all reflect a shell of a strategy without much meat or content.	A great strategy can be designed on a plain piece of paper, and a terrible strategy can be displayed using the grandest most professional looking documents. Don't be fooled by the outer package. There is nothing wrong with professional, attractive, and eye-pleasing displays for documents and tools – as long as it is understood that the content is what matters, and not the exterior packaging.

Honolulu Surfers: Data Challenges

As discussed in Chapter 8, the Honolulu Surfers organization had decided that quarterly progress reviews would be conducted in order to monitor progress toward annual goals. Fortunately, the first quarter expectations were managed by calling the new approach to measuring progress a "pilot." This was essentially a test period to see if the measures were the right fit for collection by those responsible and provided the information needed to made decisions for rudder adjustments.

As described, some middle management had difficulty fully supporting the strategy at first. Link that to the "storming" that was occurring as a natural part of team development. And, at the same time, a new measurement system was put in place. That was a lot for the Surfers' organization to manage.

Naturally, the Surfers experienced some data timeliness issues, and pockets of insufficient attention to detail. In response, staff members, coaches, and managers were asked to participate in facilitated sessions to discuss the concerns and root causes for late reporting of metrics and data that appeared to have errors. A pilot period is intended for such discussions. These discussions revealed that there were a few mismatches with data due dates and data availability. These were fixed by aligning due dates with the timing that data became available. Some managers were comfortable enough to share their misgivings on the new approach and expectations. They were assured that their voices would be heard, but would still be held accountable for timely and accurate data. Success was an organizational effort, and the Surfers were a family. The consistent support coupled with accountability and leadership engagement resolved the early issues associated with data.

SPADES SELF-ANALYSIS CHECKLIST

Instructions. After each of the challenges listed in Figure 10.1, check the appropriate column as it applies to your organization. The columns are:

SPADES Self-Analysis Checklist

Instructions: After each of the pitfalls listed below, check the appropriate column as it applies to your organization. The columns are: It is **always** there; **sometimes** we have the problem; and **never** in this organization. When you've finished the checkmarks, multiply the **always** column frequency of checkmarks by 1, the **sometimes** frequency of check marks by 3, and the **never** frequency of check marks by 5. The highest score is 105 which is a world class strategy planning organization.

Challenge	Always	Sometimes	Never
Strategy			
1-1: Lack of Strategic Focus			
1-2: SPADES Process not followed methodically			
1-3: Strategic Planning Becomes a Science Project			
1-4: Strategic Planning Becomes Stagnant and the Process Becomes Intransigent			
Leadership			
2-1: Unrealistic Vision, Mission, Goals or Objectives			
2-2: Incorrect Focus			
2-3: Disingenuous Participation by Leadership			
2-4: Lack of Clear Guidance			
2-5: Repetition Expecting Different Results			
2-6: Deployment is Stalled			
2-7: Ineffective Review Process			
2-8: Rewards and Recognition Not Commensurate with Accomplishments			
Personnel			
3-1: False Employee Engagement			
3-2: Storming			
3-3: Warring Factions			
3-4: Inflexibility			
3-5: Saboteurs			
Data			
4-1: Lack of Timely, Relevant or Accurate Data			
4-2: Insufficient Attention to Detail			
4-3: Metrics are not useful for evaluating progress			
4-4: Form over substance			

FIGURE 10.1
SPADES Self-Analysis Check-List.

It is **always** there; **sometimes** we have the problem; and **never** in this organization. When you've finished the checkmarks, multiply the **always** column frequency of checkmarks by 1, the **sometimes** frequency of check marks by 3, and the **never** frequency of check marks by 5. The highest score is 105 which is a world class strategy planning organization. This analysis will assist in identifying challenges that need to be addressed.

Honolulu Surfers: Self-Analysis Checklist

Prior to initiating SPADES, the Honolulu Surfers' leadership conducted a self-analysis using the SPADES Self-Analysis Checklist. The starting score was 55, as shown in Figure 10.2. At the end of year one implementation of SPADES, the SPADES Self-Analysis Checklist was revised, as shown in Figure 10.3. With a score of 97, there was still room to improve. And improve they did!

Challenge	Always	Sometimes	Never
Strategy			
1-1: Lack of Strategic Focus		a	
1-2: SPADES Process not followed methodically	a		
1-3: Strategic Planning Becomes a Science Project			a
1-4: Strategic Planning Becomes Stagnant and the Process Becomes Intransigent	a		
Leadership			
2-1: Unrealistic Vision, Mission, Goals or Objectives	a		
2-2: Incorrect Focus	a		
2-3: Disingenuous Participation by Leadership		a	
2-4: Lack of Clear Guidance	a		
2-5: Repetition Expecting Different Results		a	
2-6: Deployment is Stalled		a	
2-7: Ineffective Review Process		a	
2-8: Rewards and Recognition Not Commensurate with Accomplishments		a	
Personnel			
3-1: False Employee Engagement		a	
3-2: Storming		a	
3-3: Warring Factions		a	
3-4: Inflexibility		a	
3-5: Saboteurs		a	
Data			
4-1: Lack of Timely, Relevant or Accurate Data		a	
4-2: Insufficient Attention to Detail		a	
4-3: Metrics are not useful for evaluating progress		a	
4-4: Form over substance		a	

FIGURE 10.2

Honolulu Surfers' SPADES Self-Analysis Check-List (1).

Challenge	Always	Sometimes	Never
Strategy			
1-1: Lack of Strategic Focus			a
1-2: SPADES Process not followed methodically			a
1-3: Strategic Planning Becomes a Science Project			a
1-4: Strategic Planning Becomes Stagnant and the Process Becomes Intransigent			a
Leadership			
2-1: Unrealistic Vision, Mission, Goals or Objectives			a
2-2: Incorrect Focus			a
2-3: Disingenuous Participation by Leadership		a	
2-4: Lack of Clear Guidance			a
2-5: Repetition Expecting Different Results			a
2-6: Deployment is Stalled			a
2-7: Ineffective Review Process			a
2-8: Rewards and Recognition Not Commensurate with Accomplishments			a
Personnel			
3-1: False Employee Engagement			a
3-2: Storming		a	
3-3: Warring Factions			a
3-4: Inflexibility			a
3-5: Saboteurs			a
Data			
4-1: Lack of Timely, Relevant or Accurate Data		a	
4-2: Insufficient Attention to Detail		a	
4-3: Metrics are not useful for evaluating progress			a
4-4: Form over substance			a

FIGURE 10.3
Honolulu Surfers' SPADES Self-Analysis Check-List (2).

11

Epilogue

Within five years of the first steps taken by the Senior Stakeholders (Owner, Vice Presidents, Managers, and Coaches) in the Honolulu Surfers' organization to develop a sound, long-term strategy, and the agreement to participate in that first Strategy Planning Offsite, the ultimate victory was achieved. The Honolulu Surfers professional baseball franchise was crowned WORLD CHAMPIONS – IN PARADISE! The road was not an easy one. The focus on long-term planning took a leap of faith, engagement by all levels of the organization, consistent management across the board, and hard work by the players and coaches. The waves of success begot more success.

At the end of year one, when progress was reported during the Annual Review, it was evident that the enhanced hand signals that had been developed for the pitching staff were not enough to propel the team forward to win more games in year two. Thanks to the data provided by pitching coaches, and graphical representations of information using a Pareto Chart and Cause and Effect Analysis, management was easily convinced that additions to the pitching staff would further support success. The decision was made to use the newly developed affiliates to find three up-and-coming pitchers. After additional pitchers were signed to support games and practices, the Honolulu Surfers' success streak continued.

The steady tracking and achievement of actions to reach short-term objectives, followed by one- and two-year goals, and winning the league pennant resulted in a ground-swell of committed fans and players. By the

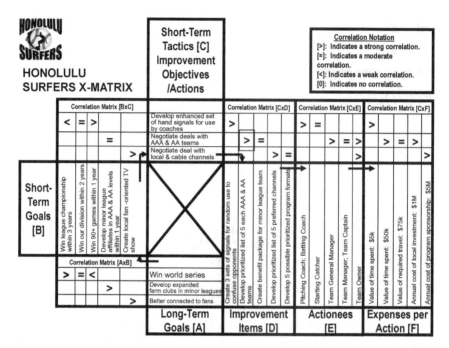

FIGURE 11.1
Honolulu Surfers' X-Matrix.

end of year two, the Surfers had rocketed not only to their goal of winning the division, but also their league – one year ahead of schedule! (See Figure 11.1.)

This rapid rise to the top surprised nearly everyone, except for those responsible. During one of countless interviews by the stream of incredulous sports reporters, the Owner, Jack S. Harrisan, found himself providing the familiar explanation: "We developed a sound strategy, and never wavered from the plan, except for the occasional adjustment." When asked how anyone knew when and where to adjust, the answer was clear and simple: "Data."

By using the SPADES approach, combining and organization's strategic approach with the plan–do–check–act model, the Honolulu Surfers' organization was able to establish an organization vision, develop long-term goals and supporting objectives, deploy and implement the plan, conduct progress and annual reviews, and make adjustments based on progress and data. The vision remained steady. The organization was aligned to reach that vision. The rest is history, fictional history in this case. *Your* story, on the other hand, is the real one. We challenge you to embrace the SPADES approach, to see where it leads you.

Appendix A

SPADES Summary

We have covered the Seven Steps of SPADES over multiple chapters. We have followed the Honolulu Surfers' professional baseball organization from its initial strategic planning efforts to an intermediate strategy engagement. In this appendix we provide a summary of the SPADES methodology. In addition, potential tools for implementing SPADES are presented to help facilitators plan for leading the development and discussions associated with the key features of each step.

STEP 1: ESTABLISH ORGANIZATIONAL VISION

Every organization needs a clear, long-term vision of what it wants to be. Management is responsible for developing this vision. The Vision Statement should be developed with input and information drawn from various constituencies within an organization. Vision statements draw an entire enterprise towards appropriate changes so as to attain its long-term vision.

TABLE A.1

Establish Organization Vision

Key Elements	Key Tools
• Data input from internal and external performance	• *Brainstorming* around issues in the external environment
• Customer focused	• *Affinity Diagram* to identify patterns among seemingly unrelated factors
• Includes all environmental factors, e.g., social, regulatory, economic, etc.	• *Market Research* technology to obtain data on external environment
• Draft of vision reviewed with organization for reality check	• *Interrelationship Digraph* to identify bottleneck factors in environment
• Finalized vision communicated clearly to everyone at all levels	

STEP 2: DEVELOP LONG-TERM GOALS

By looking at least three to five years ahead, the organization can develop long-term goals to help everyone move along the path toward the Vision. These goals should be challenging, should stretch people's comfort levels and help to ensure the organization doesn't become complacent in "the way we have always done things." In some models, this step is eliminated with the process shifting to a one-year focus immediately.

TABLE A.2

Develop Long-Term Goals

Key Elements	Key Tools
• Focus on "gap" between present organizational capability and required performance to reach vision • Accurate data from past performances determines present capability of organization and means to be pursued over next three to five years • Communicate the long-term goals clearly to everyone at all levels	• *Market Research* technology to gather data to identify midterm environmental issues • *Broad Internal Performance Reports and Analysis*, e.g., customer complaints and market share • Data collection and analysis using the *7-QC tools* • *Interrelationship Digraph* to identify most serious problem areas • *Matrix Diagram* to compare potential action plans with vision statement and criteria

STEP 3: DEVELOP SHORT-TERM AND IMMEDIATE OBJECTIVES

Annual objectives are the short-term goals that provide the action for reaching the longer-term goals. This proven, logical, methodical approach guides the organization to its destination as described by the Vision and long-term goals.

TABLE A.3

Develop Short-Term and Immediate Objectives

Key Elements	Key Tools
• Annual objectives are completely integrated with long-term goals and vision	• *Market Research* technology to identify key short-term external environmental factors
• Small number of focus points, "fewer more important efforts vs. more, more, more ..."	• *Data collection and analysis* to identify broad internal performance problems, e.g., customer complaints and profit center information
• Accurate data, minimally filtered is basis for selecting one-year objective	• *7-QC tools* to analyze and summarize key problem areas. In a mature TQM organization, these would be in use everywhere
• "Reason for improvement" must be compelling, convincing case must be made to work on any selected objective rather than on something else	• *Tree diagram* to explore every possible means to address key problem areas
	• *Matrix of all of possible means* with broad target areas for year to choose best means to pursue

STEP 4: DEPLOY/ROLL DOWN TO DEPARTMENTS TO DEVELOP PLANS

Everyone at all levels of the organization has a responsibility for intentional and specified actions that lead to achieving objectives that have been developed by leadership. A solid approach to deployment of the strategy ensures all functions are collaborative and supportive in implementing the strategic plan.

TABLE A.4

Deploy/Roll Down to Departments to Develop Plans

Key Elements	Key Tools
• Clear, disciplined action plans with direction of improvement, what is to be measured, and process to be improved	• *Matrix Diagram* to match key departments/functions with chosen objectives and means
• Continuous give and take (catchball) between levels, around chosen targets and organization's capabilities	• *7-QC Tools and Problem-Solving Models* at all involved levels to identify more specific problem areas to address
• Emphasize the plans of departments/units vs. just individuals	• *Tree Diagram* to identify all possible actions at all involved levels
• Team coordinates plans across departments	• *Matrix Diagram* to match possible actions with overall objectives to choose best options
• Responsibilities clearly designated	
• The leadership team, with assistance from SPADES facilitators, also ensures the sum of plans are collaborative and supportive for achieving the vision	

STEP 5: IMPLEMENTATION

If the plan is not implemented the work accomplished in Steps 1–4 is *wasted*. Furthermore, monitoring and measurement are critical for managing implementation. The initiation of Implementation is a perfect time for top management, or even the CEO, to engage directly with employees ensuring the official kickoff of the new strategy is given the attention and support that is essential for success. Implementation not only means enacting the plans that have been established, but also measuring progress. Monitoring and measuring provide evidence of progress as well as providing data for developing corrective action and adjusting to maintain progress to the plan. The lack of timely monitoring, measuring, and reporting progress will result in the organization losing interest and ultimate failure.

TABLE A.5

Implementation

Key Elements	Key Tools
• Disciplined data collection and measurement system implemented "in process," not after fact	• *7-QC Tools* in use to collect data as year's plan progresses
• Visible process (targets and means) allows for real-time recognition and re-enforcement	• *Process Decision Program Chart (PDPC)* to anticipate likely implementation problems and prepare reasonable means to prevent them
• Standardized methods reduce some manager-to-manager variability in outcomes	• *Arrow Diagram* to create implementation timetable against which to monitor results
• Problems are visible; therefore, management can place support where needed	

STEP 6: PROGRESS REVIEW

When deploying the strategy, all actions are linked to one or a few key metrics. The organization must be able to assess progress toward goals and objectives. A good measurement system is automatic and burdensome. It becomes a regular part of daily activities without detracting from the task at hand. Formal progress reviews, to include review of metrics, often take place on a monthly or quarterly basis in order to detect and address issues well before an annual review. Informal progress reviews may take place more frequently.

TABLE A.6

Progress Review

Key Elements	Key Tools
• Strong emphasis on self-diagnosis of targets and process	• *7-QC Tools* to define why target and plan were not met. Emphasize *Cause and Effect Diagram*, *Trend* and *Pareto Charts*
• Standardized review format and language	• Simple documents to record any changes to the plan
• Simple analysis emphasized	
• Builds plan–do–check–act continuously into process	• *Tree Diagram* to develop revised plans with complete implementation detail
• Problems are seen as opportunities to be surfaced, not skeletons to be buried	
• Emphasizes recognition, support, and corrective action, not punishment	
• System problems not directly related to plan have a place to surface	

STEP 7: ANNUAL REVIEW

The final SPADES step is the formal Annual Review. If all has gone as intended, this will be a highly anticipated event: a chance to bring all results together to show how the orchestrated plan has succeeded. Progress reviews and course corrections that take place in SPADES Step 6 should significantly reduce or eliminate the number of surprises that arise during the annual review.

TABLE A.7

Annual Review

Key Elements	Key Tools
• Data collection and review done all year providing accurate and relevant diagnosis of targets and processes, both good and bad	• *7-QC Tools* as format used to summarize results of all plans for entire year. Emphasis on answering question: Why did we miss any of our targets or plans?
• Examine plans even when target is hit, to show correlation	• *Affinity Diagram* to help identify all reasons for success or failure and any pattern which may emerge that can improve next year's planning
• Communicate results	
• Celebrate and get ready for an even better year	
• Review SPADES process itself aiming to improve it for next year	

For further details on the SPADES steps, review Chapters 6 through 8. Also, the key tools mentioned in this summary are commonplace in the Strategic Planning and Quality Management community of practice. Countless books are available to address the details of such tools.

Appendix B

Potential Tools to Use with SPADES

Throughout this book, tools have been used to serve as visual aids and to provide support in the areas of decision making, status reporting, communication, marketing, etc. As mentioned previously, many of the tools in this book are common in the Strategic Planning and Quality Management community of practice. The tools for supporting the implementation of SPADES are described in this appendix; they are listed in Table B.1.

TABLE B.1

Potential Tools to Use with SPADES

1. Affinity Diagram	12. Pareto Chart
2. Arrow Diagram	13. Performance Dashboard
3. Catchball Model	14. PERT Chart
4. Cause and Effect Analysis	15. Process Decision Program Chart
5. Current State Analysis	16. Project Selection Matrix
6. Force Field Analysis	17. Risk Management Matrix
7. Future State Estimate	18. Run Chart
8. Interrelationship Digraph	19. Senior Management Review Checklist
9. Kano Model	20. Strategy Deployment Tools
10. Organizational Chart	21. SWOT Analysis
11. Organizational Needs Matrix	22. X-Matrix Tool

1 AFFINITY DIAGRAM

The Affinity Diagram is a very effective tool for organizing language data into groupings and determining the key ideas or common themes. The results can then be used for further analysis in the planning process.

Uses of the Affinity Diagram

1. Finding a starting point for promoting new policies by creating a consensus among the group/team.
2. Invigorating project teams within groups.
3. Establishing idea conception points for the development and improvement of system products.
4. Determining trends and patterns among language data.
5. Refining and defining language data.

Title 1	Title 2	Title 3	Title 4	Title 5	Title 6
Idea A1	Idea D2	Idea A2	Idea E4	Idea A4	Idea A5
Idea B1	Idea B3	Idea B2	Idea D5	Idea A3	Idea A6
Idea C1	Idea D4	Idea D3	Idea B4	Idea F5	Idea F4
Idea D1		Idea E2	Idea E3	Idea F2	Idea F3
		Idea E1		Idea E5	
		Idea F1			

FIGURE B.1
Affinity Diagram.

2 ARROW DIAGRAM

The Arrow Diagram represents activities by arrows connected by nodes. Each node (circle) is a start or finish event. The finish node for one event is the start node of another event.

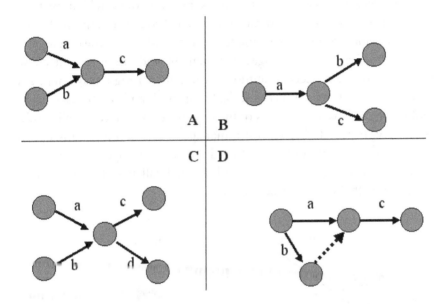

FIGURE B.2
Arrow Diagram.

3 CATCHBALL MODEL

This model represents continuous give and take ("catchball") between levels, around chosen targets and an organization's capabilities. While managers at various levels of the organization may initially draft actions for their departments and/or employees, by using the catchball method, those actions can be refined and improved through a combined effort between managers and subject matter experts (SMEs, i.e., the employees). The catchball approach engages management and employees. It allows managers to retain decision authority while increasing engagement and input from employees. This is a scalable approach and can be used across multiple as well as single levels of the organization. The catchball Model, as simply pictured, begins with management planning, "tossed" to employees for input, and then "tossed" back to management for agreement or adjustment. Another round of catchball may be used until a solid plan with SME consensus is settled.

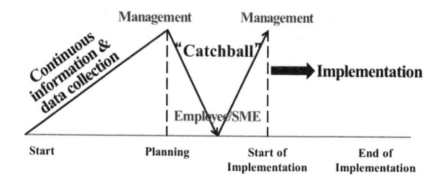

FIGURE B.3
Catchball Model.

4 CAUSE AND EFFECT ANALYSIS

The Cause and Effect Analysis uses diagramming techniques to identify the relationship between an effect and its cause. Cause and effect diagrams are also known as fishbone diagrams because they resemble the skeleton of a fish.

In order to create the fishbone diagram, the main effect is placed at the center left or right of the diagram. General categories are named and represent the main "bones of the fish." Causes of the effect are then documented and placed in the area of the appropriate category. Further causes may be identified drilling down to a greater level of detail. Once the cause cannot be broken down further, it is suggested that the analysis may have reached a "root cause." Once the root causes are addressed, then the affect should be resolved.

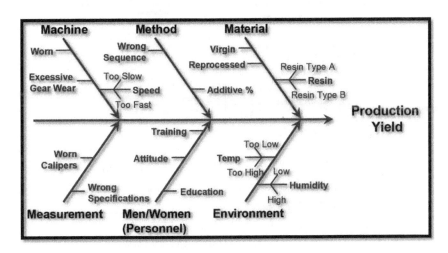

FIGURE B.4
Cause and Effect Analysis (Fishbone Diagram).

5 CURRENT STATE ANALYSIS

Current State Analysis is a tool that summarizes the current situation of an organization. It answers a set of questions regarding the current organizational environment and organizational relationships. It is the pre-cursor to the Future State Estimate. Both tools are used to establish the foundation for discussing where the organization resides today and the best path to take in order to reach a desired future state.

HONOLULU SURFER ORGANIZATION SIMPLIFIED CURRENT STATE ANALYSIS	
ORGANIZATIONAL ENVIRONMENT	
(1) Product Offerings	
What are your main product offerings?	Entertainment, Advertising Revenue, Merchandise
What is the relative importance of each to your success?	50%, 25%, 25%
What mechanisms do you use to deliver your products?	Live, Television, Streamed Video, On-line, Brick-and-Mortar Stores, Supplier to External Stores
(2) Mission, Vision, and Values	
What are your stated mission, vision, and values?	Mission: Honolulu Surfers, Winning games and riding the wave into the hearts of our loyal fans.
	Vision: We will surf the pipeline all the way to the World Series.
	Values: Fans first. Hang loose. Strong and steady.
What are your organization's core competencies, and what is their relationship to your mission?	Strong defense (pitching and fielding). Steady offense (batting and running).
(3) Workforce Profile	
What is your workforce profile?	See Figures in Chapter 1.
What recent changes have you experienced in workforce composition or in your needs with regard to your workforce?	New farm team and pitching staffs.
What are your workforce or employee groups and segments, the educational requirements for different employee groups and segments, and the key drivers that engage them in achieving your mission and vision?	See Figures in Chapter 1.
(4) Assets	
What are your major facilities, technologies, and equipment?	Surfer Stadium, Television and Cable agreements, Fan stores, and contracts with External Stores
(5) Regulatory Requirements	
What is the regulatory environment under which you operate?	MLB regulatory requirements, Salary caps, OSHA
ORGANIZATIONAL RELATIONSHIPS	
(1) Organizational Structure	
What are your organizational leadership structure and governance system?	See Figures and discussion in Chapter 1.
What are the reporting relationships among your governance board, senior leaders, and parent organization, as appropriate?	See Figures and discussion in Chapter 1.
(2) Customers and Stakeholders	
What are your key market segments, customer groups, and stakeholder groups, as appropriate?	Fans, Owners, and Advertisers
What are their key requirements and expectations for your products, customer support services, and operations?	Win games, win hearts, and grow fan base in order to grow revenue.
What are the differences in these requirements and expectations among market segments, customer groups, and stakeholder groups?	All involve increasing fan base in order to increase attendance, viewership, and merchandise sales.
(3) Suppliers and Partners	
What are your key types of suppliers, partners, and collaborators?	Honolulu Surfers organization, Farm Team organizations, MLB, broadcasters, advertisers, fans.
What are your key mechanisms for two-way communication with suppliers, partners, and collaborators?	Contracts and agreements.

FIGURE B.5
Current State Analysis.

6 FORCE FIELD ANALYSIS

This tool is used to document the forces of change and their velocity that will impact the organization in the future. The diagram shows those forces that will positively and negatively impact the organization and their velocity of change.

HOW?	WHY?	POSITIVE		NEGATIVE	WHY?	HOW?
			F O R C E S O F C H A N G E			
		STRENGTH (L, M, H)		STRENGTH (L, M, H)		

FIGURE B.6
Force Field Analysis.

The left side of Figure B.6 is where the positive forces of change are listed. Positive forces of change are ones the organization can use to drive or facilitate the strategic direction. Negative forces of change are listed on the right side of the matrix and are ones that will restrain or inhibit the organization from reaching its future desired strategic direction. Each force of change listed should be evaluated as to its strength using a scale such as high, medium, or low (H, M, or L). The high positive strength forces of change can be utilized to drive the organization forward and should be capitalized upon wherever possible in the organization. The high negative strength forces of change may require investment of organizational resources to overcome or minimize their impact on the strategic plan. The medium forces of negative change may only need to be monitored to ensure they do not become stronger. The impact of medium positive and negative forces of change upon the organization will vary from organization to organization and industry to industry. The monitoring process will also vary. The low positive forces of change are enablers to the strategic plan and should be incorporated into the organization deployment wherever possible. The low negative forces of change are usually easy to overcome and just represent a minor obstacle to the organization's progress.

7 FUTURE STATE ESTIMATE

The Future State Estimate (see Figure B.7) is a tool used to summarize the future plans and desires of an organization. This tool answers a set of questions associated with organizational change management. This summary, along with the Current State Analysis provides the basis for the preliminary planning tools for leadership prior to engaging the organization during the strategic planning.

HONOLULU SURFER ORGANIZATION SIMPLIFIED FUTURE STATE ESTIMATE	
What are the underlying factors driving the organization into the future?	Fan base growth, resulting in revenue growth.
What are current factors that work for the organization today that might change? How much and in what direction (positive and negative)?	Farm teams and pitching staffs have adequate results, but we are looking into making changes to improve standings.
What are the consequences of underestimating future trends?	May miss opportunities to acquire new talent: players and staff.
What technological changes could have the most impact and what will it cost to meet those challenges?	Transmission and relaying of games and highlights will change with technology. Important, but secondary is sales technology for fan gear.
Who will be major competitors in the future and what are their strengths and weaknesses?	Current champions will continue to be major competitors, but aging players and salary caps are weaknesses for them, while strengths for Surfers (with younger players, smaller salaries).
Who will be customers and what will they demand?	Customers demand increasing trend in winning; access to transmission of games and highlights; variety and quality of fan gear.
What workforce competencies will be required and what is the gap between current workforce competencies and the future need?	Build stronger coaching staff; seek steady source and better processes than other teams for identification of new talent.
How will these trends be monitored, and will be the reaction to any changes?	Measurement of spring training and actual results.

FIGURE B.7
Future State Estimate.

8 INTERRELATIONSHIP DIGRAPH

The Interrelationship Digraph is an effective tool for understanding the relationships among ideas and for mapping the sequential connections between them. The usual input for the Interrelationship Digraph is the result of an affinity diagram, although it can be used to analyze a set of ideas without first developing an affinity diagram.

The information developed from the Interrelationship Digraph is used to establish priorities and to determine optimum sequencing of actions.

Most commonly, an Interrelationship Digraph is set up by organizing a set of information in a vertical list and also in a horizontal list. A simple measurement scale (9 = High/3 = Medium/1 = low/blank = 0) is used to represent the relationship between any two items in the list. Paired combinations are scored and values are totaled to identify the items that have strong relationships and those that do not.

Goal: Design and Develop Training System

Is it critical to…? (columns) / **In order to…** (rows)

Column key (1–13):
1. Provide for identifying & conducting re-training as req.
2. Provide effective training methods & materials
3. Establish a formalized training system
4. Provide consistent product training throughout the company
5. Provide traceability online
6. Training required for all levels
7. Provide training reality
8. Provide evaluation of training, trainee & trainers
9. Provides training tied to performance metrics
10. What training metrics should be used?
11. Provide cross-functional awareness training
12. Training needs to include "why" purpose & where it fits in.
13. Training methods should include workshops, on-line and OJT

In order to…	1	2	3	4	5	6	7	8	9	10	11	12	13	Total
Provide for identifying & conducting re-training as req.			3		1	3			9		3	3		22
Provide effective training methods & materials			9	9	9	9		9	9				9	63
Establish a formalized training system	3	9		9	1	3		3	9	1	3	1	9	60
Provide consistent product training throughout the company	3	9	9			3	3	9	9	3	3	3	3	61
Provide traceability online	3	9	9											12
Training required for all levels	9	9	9	3	1		1	3	9		3	3	3	50
Provide training reality	9	1	9	3	1	3								36
Provide evaluation of training, trainee & trainers	1		3	9	1	3			3	3				28
Provides training tied to performance metrics	1	3	3	3		1	3	3		1	1	1		16
What training metrics should be used?	3	9	3	3		1		1				3		20
Provide cross-functional awareness training	3	1	3	1		1	3	9						19
Training needs to include "why" purpose & where it fits in.			9	3		1	1						3	14
Training methods should include workshops, on-line and OJT		9	9	3	9	9	3		3		3			54
Total	**35**	**59**	**69**	**43**	**23**	**37**	**20**	**37**	**51**	**23**	**16**	**15**	**27**	

FIGURE B.8
Interrelationship Digraph.

9 KANO MODEL

The Kano Model, as described in Figure B.9, is a tool used to graph customer needs and wants, increasing understanding from the limited descriptions provided by customers, to a more in-depth assessment based on three levels as documented by the model. The first and most basic level is known as the "Expected" level, and is the minimum description of customer needs, usually addressing reliability and durability needs. The second level is the "Wants" and addresses issues of performance of the product or service provided. This is an area where the organization can begin to differentiate itself from the competition. The third level is the "Exciting" level, where an organization builds in features or functions not expected by a customer, delivering superior performance when compared to the competition. While a baseline Kano model is useful, it is important to understand that over time, Exciting migrates to Wants and then finally to Expected. Kano Models must be updated on a regular basis due to the changes in customer needs and wants, and also the competitive environment. The classification system of the Kano Model can be used when preparing for the strategic planning session, as a way to compare and contrast the organization's performance compared to its competitors in each category.

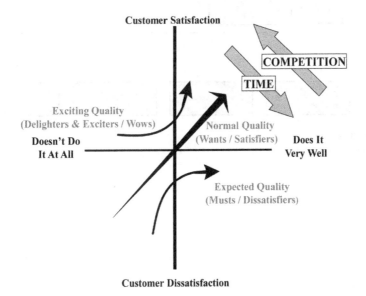

FIGURE B.9
Kano Model.

10 ORGANIZATIONAL CHART

An Organizational Chart is a visual representation of the positions and functions within an organization. Typically, the executive leader appears at the top of the chart. Each successive position is at the next level below the executive, and so on. Each position is given its own box in the diagram, to include title and possibly description of position. Lines are drawn on the diagram to depict reporting, responsible, and/or chain-of-command relationships.

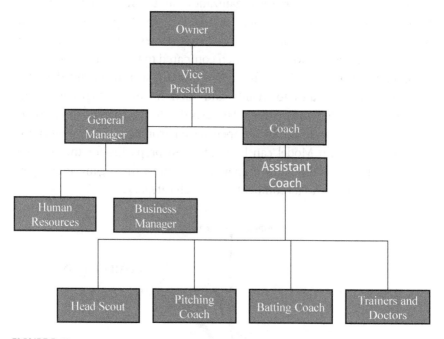

FIGURE B.10
Organizational Chart.

11 ORGANIZATIONAL NEEDS MATRIX

The Organizational Needs Matrix summarizes the organization's most pressing organizational needs. In addition to articulating and documenting the most pressing needs, the matrix shows how those pressing organizational needs are impacting the following:

- People – the organization's employees
- Processes – the primary processes of the organization
- Performance – improving efficiency and effectiveness of the organization
- Culture – creating a cohesive and aligned organization
- Morale – improving attitudes and satisfaction of employees, i.e., esprit de corps
- Customers – improving satisfaction of customers
- Other categories relevant to your organization.

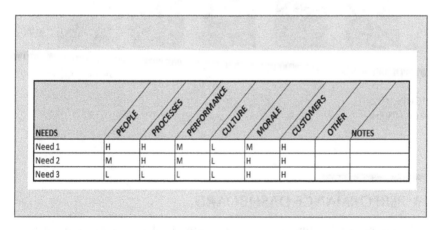

NEEDS	PEOPLE	PROCESSES	PERFORMANCE	CULTURE	MORALE	CUSTOMERS	OTHER	NOTES
Need 1	H	H	M	L	M	H		
Need 2	M	H	M	L	H	H		
Need 3	L	L	L	L	H	H		

FIGURE B.11
Organizational Needs Matrix.

The matrix includes a rating scale (such as high, medium, or low) so the impact of each need can be assessed. Comments to support each rating are captured in the matrix in the "Notes" column. It is important to understand and document the rationale for each rating.

12 PARETO CHART

A Pareto Chart is also used to visually display data. In this case, quantities are totaled by category and placed in descending order. The x-axis lists each category being measured, in descending order as defined by the data. The y-axis represents the quantity in each category. In this case, the quantity is in the form of percentage of the overall goal.

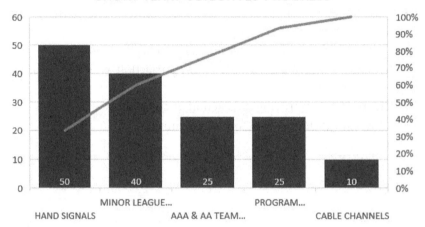

FIGURE B.12
Pareto Chart.

13 PERFORMANCE DASHBOARD

A Performance Dashboard is an excellent tool for displaying multiple items of data and graphics in a single location. Dashboards are often used by leadership or communities, and must be developed so that they are easily understood with minimal explanation needed. Dashboards should also be kept up-to-date so that current information is visible and can be used for decisions and action planning.

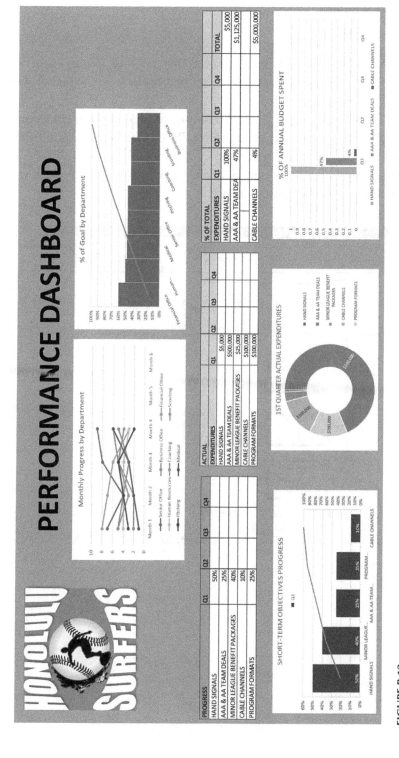

FIGURE B.13
Performance Dashboard.

14 PERT CHART

Program Evaluation and Review Technique (PERT) charts were first developed to help manage very large, complex projects with a high degree of inter-task dependency.

PERT is a Planning and Control tool used for defining and controlling the tasks necessary to complete a project. PERT Charts and Critical-Path Method (CPM) charts are often used interchangeably; the only difference is how task times are computed. Both charts display the total Project with all scheduled tasks shown in sequence.

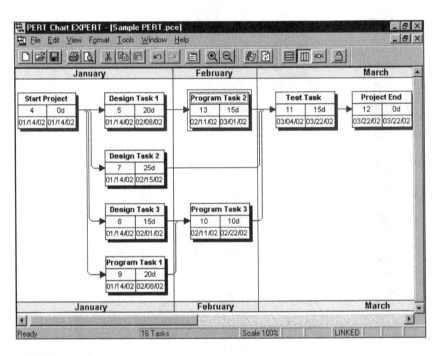

FIGURE B.14
PERT Chart.

15 PROCESS DECISION PROGRAM CHART

The Process Decision Program Chart (PDPC) is a tool that assists in anticipating events and in developing counter-measures for undesired occurrences. The PDPC is typically used when:

1. A task is unique
2. The situation is complex
3. The price of potential failure is unacceptable.

The PDPC is similar to the tree diagram. It leads you through the identification of the tasks and paths necessary to achieve a goal and its associated sub-goals. The PDPC then leads you to answer the questions "What could go wrong?" and "What unexpected events could occur?" Next, by providing effective contingency planning, the PDPC leads to developing appropriate countermeasures.

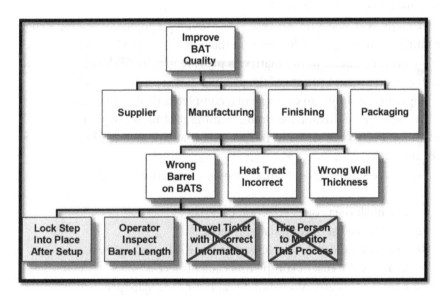

FIGURE B.15
Process Decision Program Chart.

16 PROJECT SELECTION MATRIX

The Project Selection Matrix makes the identification, selection, and prioritization of projects more objective and easier to validate. By adopting this matrix, key management-driven (top-down) projects can be more easily identified and approved by the senior management team.

The selection process provides a straightforward way to gather the appropriate data from all areas of the business, segregate by improvement categories and apply a rating for prioritization. The frustrations, issues, problems, and opportunities visible inside the company are key sources of potential projects.

The process for developing the matrix clarifies the relationships between the means and the goals, thus ensuring that all of the customers' requirements are addressed. "Goal" is used to denote "what" is to be achieved, and "means" refers to "how" it is to be achieved. In a matrix, we list the goals on the vertical axis as the "whats," and the means on the horizontal axis as the "hows."

This project selection process also provides a logical basis for determining the impact of each action on the other actions. Optional enhancements can be added to the matrix to provide greater understanding, and to facilitate the next phases of the product development project.

Figure B.16 shows an example of a completed Project Selection Matrix. This matrix is an invaluable brainstorming tool to assist your team with aligning limited resources to the projects that will give the biggest "bang for the buck."

There are six steps to creating the project selection matrix:

1. Establish the project selection criteria.
2. Establish a list of candidate projects.
3. Evaluate candidate projects against the selection criteria.
4. Evaluate the risk of completing each project.
5. Create an interrelationship digraph for candidate projects.
6. Prioritize and select a project.

Risk:
1 = weak
3 = Moderate
9 = High

Evaluation Criteria / Candidate Projects	Reduce Production Scrap Rate	Improve Supplier Management	Improve Delivery Schedule	Increase System Performance to 6σ Level	Reduce Mechanical Interfaces	Change Integration Strategy; Outsource Hi-Tech	Total
Reduce Cost of Poor Quality	9	3			3	3	18
Reduce Risk				9	9		18
Improve Cost Performance		3			9	3	15
Improve Schedule Performance		9	9	9	3	9	39
Improve System/Project Performance					9		9
Improve Rolled Through Rate	9				3	1	13
Improve Process Performance	3					3	6
Improve Completion Schedule Requirements			9				9
Support Strategic Business Goals	9	9	9	9	3	3	42
Support Program Goals	3	9	9	3	3	3	30
Improve Customer Satisfaction			9	9	9		27
Total	33	33	45	39	51	25	
Priority	5	4	2	3	1	6	
Risk	1	1	3	9	3	9	

FIGURE B.16
Project Selection Matrix.

17 RISK MANAGEMENT MATRIX

Risk analysis consists of risk identification, probability assessment, and impact estimate. Start by identifying all the risk events that can occur on your Project. Then estimate the probability of each event happening. Finally, estimate the impact in hours or dollars if the event occurs. Once you have listed and quantified the project risks, then you should prepare a risk management plan for each significant risk item. The final step would be to formalize this into a risk management activity, establish metrics, and track your top ten risks week by week.

Risk Event	Probability	Impact	Risk Score	Risk Mitigation Plan
Change host operating system	.2	100 hours	20 hours	Work with host support group
Redesign data model	.4	200 hours	80 hours	Do early prototyping
Data conversion is late	.7	300 hours	210 hours	Request tracking of progress
Total Risk:			310 hours	

FIGURE B.17
Risk Management Matrix.

18 RUN CHART

A Run Chart is used to visually display data over time. The x-axis is set up by increments of time moving from left to right. The y-axis displays the count or measurement of the data that is being displayed over time. Data points are plotted by time/quantity (x/y) with a line connecting each point, simply showing the changes over time. In this case, the data represents number of actions completed each month. The shading (or colors) distinguish individual departments.

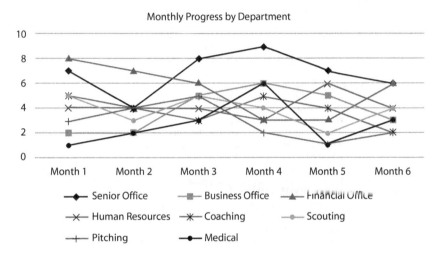

FIGURE B.18
Run Chart.

19 SENIOR MANAGEMENT REVIEW CHECKLIST

This simple checklist can be used or tailored to management needs in order to help prepare participants for annual or interim reviews of the status of strategy implementation. By using a consistent approach to conducting reviews, the organization can improve and standardize the implementation process for strategy deployment.

Senior Management Review Checklist

1. Before The Review:
   a. Familiarize yourself with the Status Reports or Plan/Delta Reports submitted
   b. Inform participants about questions to be asked
   c. Confirm time and place for the Review
   d. Send each participant a completed management review form

2. Before The Review:
   Inform participants about questions to be asked such as:
   a. To which organizational objectives are you aligned?
   b. What are your work unit objectives?
   c. What criteria did you use to choose those objectives/actions?
   d. Who is accountable for objectives being completed?
   e. Why did you choose these improvements?
   f. How will you measure them?
   g. What % completion are you at this point?
   h. Are you on plan or off plan? Why?
   i. Do you have actions detailed to get back on Plan?
   j. What additional resources might you need?
   k. What are the critical processes?
   l. Can these results be replicated elsewhere in the organization?

3. During The Review:
   a. Clarify the purpose of the Review
   b. Stick to the agenda and questions
   c. Look for the alignment of goals and objectives
   d. Ask the agreed upon questions
   e. Create a two-way dialogue and build trust
   f. Probe the goals/objectives/targets - make sure they are stretch
   g. Document agreed upon modifications and follow-up items
   h. Give everyone feedback at the end of the Review
   i. Decide on the time and place of the next Review

4. After The Review:
   a. Send out formal Feedback Report within one week
   b. Document agreements and modifications
   c. Follow-up on agreements
   d. Document obstacles that are common among all teams/participants and start to address them with Executive Level involvement
   e. Prepare notes for next Review

FIGURE B.19
Senior Manager Review Checklist.

20 STRATEGY DEPLOYMENT TOOLS

There are many tools available to assist organizations with implementing strategies. Simple examples for documenting details are the Strategy Deployment Table Worksheet (Figure B.20a) and the Strategy Deployment Table (Figure B.20b). Both are easy to understand, and can be standardized across the entire organization, allowing for ease in combining and rolling up results for reporting purposes.

Strategy Deployment Table Worksheet

Department:_____

Prepared By:_____

1. Goal or Objective being addressed:

2. Actions to support the Goal or Objective:

3. Tasks and Sub-Tasks (as applicable):

4. Who is responsible for each Action/Task:

5. Timeline to complete the action:

6. How and when the action will be measured:

7. Identify the % complete of each action at each review period.

FIGURE B.20A
Strategy Deployment Table Worksheet.

STRATEGY DEPLOYMENT TABLE

DEPARTMENT:
PREPARED BY:
LAST UPDATED:

GOAL	ACTIONS TO BE TAKEN	TASKS TO SUPPORT ACTIONS	SUB-TASKS	RESPONSIBLE PERSON	DUE DATE	MEASURE-MENT	% COMPLETE

FIGURE B.20B
Strategy Deployment Table.

21 SWOT ANALYSIS

The SWOT Analysis provides a summary of the current Strengths, Weaknesses, Opportunities, and Threats, the organization is facing. This tool is used at the beginning of a strategic planning session to gather input from everyone attending the retreat. The SWOT Analysis tool summarizing results of the planning meeting and presents it in a visual format. The SWOT Analysis is accomplished by dividing the group into teams, with each one taking one of the four categories to discuss and define the results. Each group reports their results to the other three and facilitates further discussion to develop consensus on the results.

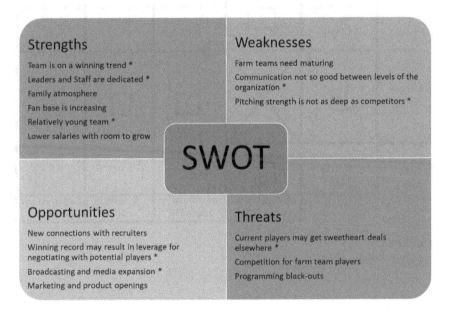

FIGURE B.21
SWOT Analysis.

22 X-MATRIX TOOL

The X-Matrix has been uniquely developed to support the SPADES approach to strategy planning. Chapter 5 of this book is dedicated to describing the use and content of this tool.

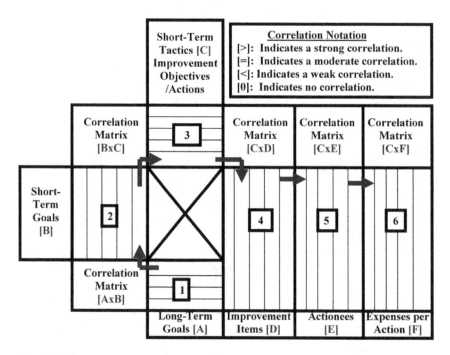

FIGURE B.22
X-Matrix Tool.

Index

Page numbers in *italics* denote figures, those in **bold** denote tables.

7-QC tools *see* Seven Quality Control
(7-QC) tools

A

accountability, 91
action items, 31–2
action notes, 31
action plans, 30, 32, 59, 71, 75, 90, **105**,
124, **126**, 144
  Honolulu Surfers, 79
action tables, 81
actionees/accountable persons, 38, 40, 42
Affinity Diagram, **123**, **129**, 131–2, *132*
annual objectives (short-term goals), 45,
50–2, 76, 86, **125**, 125
  accurate data as basis for, 51
  criteria for selecting, 51–2
  focus on essential, 51
  Honolulu Surfers, 56
  integration with long-term goals, 51
annual reviews, 45, 71–2, 75–7, 85, **129**,
129
  celebration of successes, 77, 129
  communication of results, 76–7
  Honolulu Surfers, 81–3
  Performance Dashboard, 76
  and success and failure, 76

Arrow Diagram, **127**, *133*, 133
assets, 18

B

background sessions, 26
brainstorming, **123**
briefing books, 25–6, 33
business environment, 15, 71
  changes in, 1, 85

C

cascading effect for strategic planning,
59–60
Catchball Model, *59*, 59, **99**, **126**, *134*, 134
Cause and Effect Analysis, *135*, 135
Cause and Effect Diagram (fishbone
diagram), **128**, *135*, 135
celebration of success, 77
challenge
  acceptance of, 91
  see also organizational challenges and
cures
change
  in business environment, 1, 85
  forces of, 28–30
  technological, 1, 71, 85
Chief Executive, 9, 10–11, 12
  Honolulu Surfers, 13

Collins, Jim, 51

communications, 7–8, **104**

Communications Plan, 4

competitiveness, 1

coordination across departments, 60

correlation matrices, 37, 38–9, 41

correlation symbols, 37, 39

critical functions of enterprises, 7–10

    market research, customer research, and communications, 7–8

    measurement, analysis and knowledge management, 9–10

    product and process commercialization, 8

    product, service and process design, 8

    product and service production, 8–9

    product and service support, 8–9

    research and technology development, 8

    strategic planning, 7

culture, 28, 85, 143

current state analysis, 136

    Honolulu Surfers, 23, *136*

current state assessment, 15, 16–19

    Honolulu Surfers, *22*

customer focus, 47, **123**

customer needs and wants, 15, 16, 19–20

    Honolulu Surfers, 22

    Kano Model, 19, *20*, *141*, 141

customer research and communications, 7–8

customer satisfaction, 7, 9, 20, 28, 72, 143

customer surveys, 26, 33

customers, 18, 31

D

data challenges, 97, 110–11, **112**

    form over substance, 111, **112**

    Honolulu Surfers, 113, 115

    insufficient attention to detail, 111, **112**

    lack of timely, relevant, or accurate data, 110–11, **112**

    metrics not useful for evaluating progress, 111, **112**

    preventive actions and cures, **112**

data collection, 4, 9, 47, 51, 62, **112**, **124**, **125**

data input from internal and external performance, 47, **123**

Deming, W. Edward, 64, 74

Deming-Shewhart Cycle (PDCA Cycle), 2, 74, **128**

deployment of the strategic plan, 4, 57

    deploy/roll down to departments to develop plans, 45, 58–61, **126**, 126

    Honolulu Surfers, 66–8

    monitoring of, **104**

    non-line of sight obstacles, 57

    as a process, 4

    stalled, 102, **105**

developing annual objectives *see* annual objectives

developing long-term goals *see* long-term goals

developing the strategy, 45–56

disingenuous participation by leadership, 101, **104**

E

economic environment, 47

employees, 27, 31, 73

    false engagement of, 106, **108**

    morale, 28, 101, 143

    trust, 73

    see also personnel challenges

enterprise(s)

    definitions of, 7

    see also critical functions of enterprises

environmental factors, 18, 47, **123**

    see also business environment; organizational environment; regulatory environment

error, as source of unexpected
consequences, 3
establishing organization vision, 45, 46–8,
123, 123
Executive Staff, 9, 11
Honolulu Surfers, 13
expenses per action, 38, 40, 42

F

facilitators
for SPADES, 10, 11, 12, 14, **99**
strategy review, 87
fact-based data, 18, 19
false employee engagement, 106, **108**
fishbone diagram (Cause and Effect
Diagram), **128**, *135*, 135
force field analysis, 28–30, *29*, *137*, 137–8
Honolulu Surfers, *35*, 35
Ford, Henry, 47
form over substance, 111, **112**
forming stage of group development, 106,
108, 110
future state estimate, 15, 20–1, 136, 138
Honolulu Surfers, 22, *24*, *138*

G

Goal Deployment and Alignment Model,
86
goals, 7, 10, 40
strategic plan, 30
unrealistic, 100–1, **104**
see also annual objectives (short-term
goals); long-term goals
group development, phases of, 106, **108**,
110
group think, 47, **104**

H

Honolulu Surfers, 119–20
action plans, 79
annual objectives (short-term goals), 56
annual review, 81–3
current state analysis, 23, *136*
data challenges, 113, 115
deployment of strategic plan, 66–8
force field analysis, *35*, 35
future state estimate, 22, *24*, *138*
implementation of SPADES, 4–5
Steps 1–3, 52–6
Steps 4–5, 66–70
Steps 6–7, 78–83
implementation of strategic plan, 68–70
leadership challenges, 103, 106
long-term goals, 53–5
Organizational Needs Matrix, *34*, 34
Pareto Chart, *63*, *69*, *79*
Performance Dashboard, 79, *80*, 145
personnel challenges, 107, 110
preparation for strategic planning, 22,
23, *24*
progress reviews, 78–81
reviewing and refining strategy, 92–5
Run Chart, *63*, *69*, *78*
SPADE roles and responsibilities, 12–14
SPADES Self-Analysis Checklist, 115,
116–17
strategy challenges, 100
strategy planning, 32–5
SWOT Analysis, 33, *34*
vision, 53
X-Matrix, 40–4, *41*, *42*, 43, *44*, *68*, *120*
Hoshin Kanri, 1–2

I

IBM, 48–9
implementation of SPADES, 3–4
Honolulu Surfers *see under* Honolulu
Surfers
roles and responsibilities, 10–14
implementation of strategic plan, 45, 61–5,
127, 127
Honolulu Surfers, 68–70

improvement items, 38, 40, 42
improvement objectives/actions, 2, 38
incorrect focus, 101, **104**
ineffective review process, 102–3, **105**
inflexibility, 107, **109**
information, 9
insufficient attention to detail, 111, **112**
Interrelationship Digraph, **123**, **124**, 139, *140*

K

Kano Model, 19, *20*, *141*, 141
keynote speaker address, 26
knowledge experts, 26
knowledge, lack of, 3
knowledge management, 9

L

lack of clear guidance, 102, **104**
lack of knowledge, 3
lack of strategic focus, 98, **99**
lack of timely, relevant or accurate data, 110–11, **112**
leadership, 25
leadership challenges, 97, 100–3, **104–5**, 106
    deployment is stalled, 102, **105**
    disingenuous participation by leadership, 101, **104**
    Honolulu Surfers, *103*, 106
    incorrect focus, 101, **104**
    ineffective review process, 102–3, **105**
    lack of clear guidance, 102, **104**
    preventive actions and cures, **104–5**
    repetition expecting different results, 102, **105**
    rewards and recognition not commensurate with accomplishments 103, **105**
    unrealistic vision, mission, goals or objectives, 100–1

long-term goals, 31, 38, 41, 45, 48–50, 76, 86, **124**, 124
    annual objectives integration with, 51
    communication of, 49–50, **124**
    Honolulu Surfers, 53–5
    and performance gap, 49, **124**
long-term success, 10

M

Malcolm Baldrige National Quality Award (MBNQA), 17–18
management by means, 1–2
managers, 11
    Honolulu Surfers, 13–14
market research, 7–8, **123**, **124**, **125**
Matrix Diagram, **124**, **126**
Merton, Robert, 2–3
metrics (measurement), 9, 10, 51, 62, 97, **112**
    measures of success, 72
    not useful for evaluating progress, 111, **112**
    standardized methods, 62–3
    training, 63, **112**
mission, 3, 4, 7, 10, 15, 17
    unrealistic, 100–1, **104**
mission statement, 7
morale, 28, 101, 143

N

negative trends, 62, 64
norming stage of group development, 106, **108**, 110

O

objectives, 4, 7
    organizational, 90
    short-term (annual), 45, 50–2, 76
    unrealistic, 100–1, **104**
operational leaders, 11–12
    Honolulu Surfers, 13–14

operational thinking, 21
operators, 9
opinion-based data, 18–19
organizational challenges and cures,
    97–117
    data, 97, 110–11, **112**, 113
    leadership, 97, 100–3, **104–5**, 106
    personnel, 97, 106–7, **108–9**, 110
    strategy, 97, 98, **99**, 100
Organizational Chart, *142*, 142
organizational environment, 17
    Honolulu Surfers, 23
Organizational Needs Matrix, *28*, 27–8,
    143, 143
    Honolulu Surfers, *34*, 34
organizational relationships, 18
    Honolulu Surfers, *23*
organizational structure, 18

P

Pareto Chart, 62, *79*, **128**, *144*, 144
    Honolulu Surfers, *63*, *69*, *79*
partners, 18
PDCA (plan–do–check–act), 2, 74, **128**
Performance Dashboard, 76, 144
    Honolulu Surfers, 79, *80*, *145*
performance, organizational needs impact
    on, 27, 143
performance gap, 49, **124**
performance metrics, 4, 9, 10
performance reviews, 102–3, **105**
performing stage of group development,
    106, **108**, 110
personnel challenges, 97, 106–7, **108–9**,
    110
    false employee engagement, 106, 108
    Honolulu Surfers, *107*, 110
    inflexibility, 107, **109**
    preventive actions and cures, **108–9**
    saboteurs, 107, **109**
    storming, 106, **108**, 110

warring factions, 106–7, **108**
    see also employees
PERT Chart, *146*, 146
plan–do–check–act (PDCA), 2, 74, **128**
plan of action and milestones (POA&M),
    32
potential tools to use with SPADES, 131–56
prediction, 3
preparation for strategic planning, 15–24
    current state assessment, 15, 16–19
    customer needs and wants, 15, 16,
        19–20
    future state estimate, 15, 20–1
    Honolulu Surfers, 22, *23*, *24*
Process Decision Program Chart (PDPC),
    127, 146, *147*, 147
process improvement team (PIT), 64
processes, organizational needs impact on,
    27, 143
product offerings, 17
product and process commercialization, 8
product, service and process design, 8
product and service production, 8–9
product and service support, 8–9
Program Evaluation and Review
    Technique (PERT) Chart, *146*,
    146
progress reviews, 4, 12, 45, 71–5, 90, **99**,
    105, **109**, **128**, 128
    emphasis on recognition, support,
        and corrective action, not
        punishment, 74, **128**
    emphasis on self-diagnosis of targets
        and process, 73, **128**
    emphasis on simple analysis, 73, **128**
    Honolulu Surfers, 78–81
    normal, increased, and decreased
        frequency, 73
    as opportunity for problems to be
        surfaced and resolved, 74
    and plan–do–check–act (PDCA) cycle,
        74, **128**

progress reviews *continued*
    reasons to conduct, 75
    standardized format and language, 73,
        128
    and surfacing of system problems not
        directly related to the plan, 75,
        128
Project Selection Matrix, 148, *149*

Q

quality function deployment (QFD), 2

R

recognition *see* rewards and recognition
recovery plans, 12, 72, 95, 97, **99**, **105**
refining the strategy, 91–2
    Honolulu Surfers, 92–5
regulatory environment, 18, 47
repetition expecting different results, 102,
    105
research and technology development, 8
responsibilities *see* roles and responsibilities
    review slide layout, *87*
review of strategy *see* strategy review
rewards and recognition, 74, 77
    not commensurate with
        accomplishments, 103, **105**
Risk Management Matrix, *150*, 150
roles and responsibilities, 10–12
    clear designation of, 60
    Honolulu Surfers, 12–14
    for strategy review meetings, 88–91
Run Chart, 62, *151*, 151
    Honolulu Surfers, *63*, *69*, *78*

S

saboteurs, 107, **109**
Schumpeter, Joseph, 1
scientific method, 2, 74
Seneca, 25

Senior Management Review Checklist, 88,
    89, *152*, 152
Seven Quality Control (7-QC) Tools, 62,
    124, 125, 126, 127, 128, 129
short-term goals *see* annual objectives
    (short-term goals)
short-term tactics/improvement
    objectives/actions, 38, 41, 42
silo thinking, 90
SMART actions, 59, 60, 62
social environment, 47
SPADES
    definition and rationale, 2
    facilitators, 10, 11, 12, 14, **99**
    potential tools to use with, 131–56
    process not followed methodically, 98, **99**
    roles and responsibilities, 10–14
    scientific method as foundation of, 2
SPADES Self-Analysis Checklist, 113, *114*
    Honolulu Surfers, 115, 116–17
SPADES Seven Steps
    Step 1 Establish Organization Vision,
        45, 46–8, 123, 123
    Step 2 Develop Long-Term Goals, 45,
        48–50, 124, 124
    Step 3 Develop Short-Term and
        Immediate Goals, 45, 50–2,
        125, 125
    Step 4 Deploy/Roll Down to
        Departments to Develop Plans,
        45, 58–61, **126**, 126
    Step 5 Implementation, 45, 61–5, **127**,
        127
    Step 6 Progress Review, 45, 71–5, **128**,
        128
    Step 7 Annual Review, 45, 71–2, 75–7,
        129, 129
SPADES X-Matrix, 31, 37–9, 60, 61, 64
    Honolulu Surfers, 40–4, *41*, *42*, *43*, *44*,
        68, *120*
    legend, 37–9
    template, 39, *40*

Specific, Measurable, Achievable, Relevant, and Timebound (SMART) actions, 59, 60, 62
stakeholders, 18, 30, 31
Statistical Control Chart, 62
storming stage of group development, 106, **108**, 110
strategic alignment, 60–1
strategic focus, lack of, 98, **99**
strategic plan, 7, 30–2
   communications plan, 4
   data requirements, 4
   goals, 30
   key components, 15, 30–1
   review of *see* strategy review
   SPADES as sound methodology for developing, 3
   see also deployment of the strategic plan; refining the strategy
strategic planning
   becomes a science project, 98, **99**
   becomes stagnant and the process becomes intransigent, **99**, 100
   as critical function of an enterprise, 7
   waterfall or cascading effect for, 59–60
   see also preparation for strategic planning
Strategic Planning and Development Excellence System *see* SPADES
strategy challenges, 97, 98, **99**, 100
   Honolulu Surfers, 100
   lack of strategic focus, 98, **99**
   preventive actions and cures, **99**
   SPADES process nor followed methodically, 98, **99**
   strategic planning becomes a science project, 98, **99**
   strategic planning becomes stagnant and the process becomes intransigent, **99**, 100
Strategy Deployment Table, 64, *65*, 88, *153*, *154*

Strategy Deployment Table Worksheet, 64, *65*, 88, *153*, 155
strategy planning retreat, 25–32
   Honolulu Surfers, 32–5
strategy review, 85–91
   facilitators, 87
   Honolulu Surfers, 92–5
   review of prior year accomplishments, 86–8
   roles and responsibilities for review meeting, 88–91
Strengths–Weakness–Opportunities–Threats Analysis (SWOT Analysis), 4, 27, *155*, 155
   Honolulu Surfers, 33, *34*
success
   celebration of, 77
   long-term, 10
supervisors, 9
suppliers, 18

T

tactics, 40
   short-term, 38, 41, 42
technicians, 9
technological change, 1, 71, 85
Tree Diagram, **125**, **126**, **128**
trust, 73

U

unexpected consequences, 2–3
unrealistic vision, mission, goals or objectives, 100–1, **104**

V

values, 3, 4, 7, 15, 17
vision, 3, 4, 7, 10, 15, 16, 17, 90
   communication of, 48, **123**
   establishing, 45, 46–8, **123**, 123
   Honolulu Surfers, 53
   review for reality check, 47–8, **123**
   unrealistic, 100–1, **104**

W

warring factions, 106–7, **108**
waterfall effect for strategic planning, 59–60
white boards, 76, 81
workforce profile, 17

X

X-Matrix, *156*, 156
   Honolulu Surfers, 40–4, *41*, *42*, *43*, *44*,
      68, *120*
   see also SPADES X-Matrix